The Life and Death of the Liverpool Barque *Dryad* (1874–91)

Henry G.L. Alexander
B.Sc., PhD.

Published 2004 by Aunemouth Books
Aune Cross Lodge, Bantham, Kingsbridge, Devon TQ7 3AD
01548 561182

ISBN 0-9549022-0-03

Printed and bound in Great Britain by
Short Run Press Ltd, Exeter, Devon.

ACKNOWLEDGEMENTS

Many organisations and individuals have helped me with my enquiries over the years and it is no exaggeration to say that this book would not have been possible without their assistance. Sadly some are no longer with us. My thanks to all.
Ted Albert, Alan Ashford, Mr P.R. Auldis, Mrs Nancy Batten, Bryony Chapman, Charlie Chester, Malcolm Darch, Len Fairweather, Hazel Hawkins, Mr Haydn and Mrs Mary Jenkins, Norman Lancashire, Richard Larn, Martin Leathers, David and Carole Light, David MacGregor, David Murch, Mrs Alison Palmer, Kathy Pryne, Bob Roberts, Brian Scutt, Mrs Pauline Shelley, Robert Silvester, Michael K. Stammers, The Thomas Family of Pembrokeshire, Bob Troake, Jim Trout, Alan Viner, Sharon Wellington. I offer my apologies to anyone whom I have omitted.

The British Broadcasting Corporation
Central Library, Liverpool
Cookworthy Museum, Kingsbridge
"Country Life" Magazine
Devon County Coroner
Devon Records Office
Exeter Express Post
Exeter Flying Post
Guildhall Library, Aldermanbury, EC2.
H M Customs and Excise
Lloyds of London
Lloyds Register of Shipping
"Maritime Wales"
Merseyside County Museum
Melbourne Argus
Memorial University of Newfoundland
National Maritime Museum, Greenwich
National Maritime Museum, San Francisco
National Meteorological Archives
Newspaper Library, Collindale
Public Records Office, Kew
Receiver of Wreck, Dartmouth
Receiver of Wreck, Newhaven
Scouse Press
"Sea Breezes" Magazine
South Hams Newspapers, Kingsbridge
South Wales Daily News
Salvage Association
The Liverpool Echo
Trinity House
West Devon Records Office, Plymouth

My grateful thanks are also due to Mrs Margi Hawkins who translated my scrawl and odd sheets of typing into a proper script and who dropped doing important things in her life to deal with urgent items for me.

Lastly, but by no means least, I thank my wife Vida for her encouragement and support, helpful discussion and reading over the script to spot errors, omissions and offer suggestions with phraseology.

CONTENTS

PROLOGUE

"*. . . it is doubtful if there is much surviving material relating to the Dryad . . . just another smallish wreck, and joined a very long line of smallish vessels in the area; you wouldn't expect to find that much information remaining in 100 years time . . .*

Part of a letter to the author from Richard Larn (renowned author and researcher of Shipwrecks) 19th July 1984.

DEDICATION

In memory of all my friends, both two legged and four,
who no longer walk this earth with me.

INTRODUCTION

Young Frank Smith must have been excited yet apprehensive as he sat quietly in the dim corridor at 18, Chapel Street, Liverpool. At his side was his father, who had come to witness his son's signature at the offices of J B Walmsley & Co, the shipowners. Just sixteen years old, Frank was about to sign on for a five year apprenticeship for the total sum of £30. In the first and second year he would earn £4 per annum; in the third and fourth years it would be £6, and in the fifth and final year he would earn £10. Little did he realise that within 5 weeks he would lose his life on his very first ship, wrecked in the infamous blizzard of 1891, along with 62 other ships along the southern coast of Britain. He would die with the rest of the crew of the iron barque *Dryad*, as she slammed into the cliffs of Start Point, South Devon.

The night had been dark and stormy, with fine stinging snow being driven before the north-easterly blizzard. Because of the poor visibility the helmsman would have been steering by dead reckoning; even the bright light of Start Point lighthouse would not have penetrated the storm. Perhaps the first anyone on board would have known of their imminent peril was the horrific sound of the *Dryad's* hull being wrenched apart by the rocks. Perhaps the helmsman had seen the cliffs, but too late he threw the wheel over to port in a frantic but hopeless attempt to clear the point.

The huge seas must have thrown the ship, her cargo and crew again and again against the cliffs, smashing the fine ship into a heap of iron plates in a matter of minutes. The first contact with the shallow bottom near the cliffs would have terrified Captain William Thomas and his crew, and the impact would have sent numerous items crashing to the deck. Almost certainly coals were spilt from the fire grate in the cabin and wooden fittings caught alight. Any of the sleeping watch would have awakened, and scrambled onto the wave washed decks, surely knowing their end was near.

The ship broke up rapidly, throwing all 21 crew into the boiling sea, to be repeatedly beaten against, and scrubbed up and down, the sharp barnacle-encrusted cliffs. Mercifully some may have been killed quickly, but one man at least is known to have spent a horrible night clinging frozen and terrified to a pinnacle of rock before being swept into eternity, snatched from the helping hands of the Start lighthouse keeper and some coastguards.

After the mourning, the inquest and inquiry, the event was slowly forgotten; as time heals all wounds. The seasons came and went and over the years the fragmented remains of a once proud ship were slowly eroded away. Some of her artifacts sank down into the sand and silt to form an amalgam with rust and coal, shell and stone; a natural concretion to preserve and hide the evidence of the disaster which had befallen on the night of 9/10th March 1891.

In September 1974 I came across her remains. This book is the story of what followed.

Chapter One

DISCOVERY

I had enjoyed my late summer diving holiday in Devon very much. One evening my diving buddy Doug Barnard and I were enjoying a pint in the Start Bay Inn at Torcross, when we got into conversation with a local fisherman who said that there were rumoured to be some underwater caves linking the east and west sides of Start Point. This seemed an interesting dive, so we agreed to have a look the following day. At the time the pub was owned by Laurie Emberson, now better known as an underwater natural history film maker. He came with us for the dive.

I remember it was a calm, warm, sunny afternoon as Doug, Laurie, another friend and I slipped beneath the surface some 600 yards to the north of Start Point and swam leisurely along the cliff bottom looking for the caves. The cliff base is very irregular, with many inlets and massive boulders fallen from above. Towards the end of the dive we came across some iron plates. It was not obvious what they were. They could have been fragments of a long lost ship, or some scrap discarded over the cliff by someone years before. Back on the dive boat someone said they had seen what appeared to be some pieces of wreckage sticking up several feet from the sea bed, seemingly from a ship. We thought no more of it as, heading back to the campsite with warm wind, sun and spray in our faces, the conversation centred around the menu for the evening's meal. A few more days general diving in and around the Start Bay area and it was time to return to London and work. We never did find those caves – if they ever existed at all.

In the early and mid 1970's I used to run diving courses for biologists and other interested parties at Slapton Ley Field Centre. (On a map Slapton village is about 'half way up' Start Bay). One year Kathy, the Centre's secretary, said she would like to learn to dive and, having organised the necessary leave, joined a week's course along with a number of lads. Two of the trainee divers showed a great deal of promise and were keen to forsake the swimming pool of their training and try the real thing. Kathy lived locally and suggested that later in the year the two lads and I might come down for a few days to stay with her parents and the four of us do some diving. Martin and Robert were very enthusiastic and had done a lot of reading about dives and diving over the couple of months since the course. They had purchased equipment and were itching to try it out. Their first few shallow water beach dives had convinced me that these two had all the makings of a pair of excellent divers, and I was

Plate 1
Robert and Martin over the wreck site in their inflatable.

Plate 2
"We swan leisurely along the cliff bottom . . ."

keen for them to try a few more interesting sites. My mind wandered back to the couple of summers before when I had seen those remains near Start Point. I suggested we went back and had another look.

Next day we anchored the inflatable in a convenient spot, kitted up, dropped overboard and down. There was hardly any current and, as well as being safe for beginners, the shallow water meant there was plenty of light. The visibility was good with 20 feet or more. Masses of kelp and other seaweeds waved gently to and fro as we nosed around the rocky bottom looking for those iron plates I had seen a couple of years ago. I knew we were in the right general area, but I could not locate the exact spot.

Although the predominant winds of the area drive into the west facing cliffs of Start Point, in the winter there are frequently easterly gales and these serve to erode the cliffs causing rock falls on the east side. The boulders and rock debris which rain down from above tend to accumulate on the sea bed and the agitation of the water during the storms cause the rocks to settle. This movement also helps to bury artifacts and to destroy and fragment large items. Sometimes sand and shingle seem to accumulate in the southern part of Start Bay, on other occasions it disappears. I have seen Hallsands beach almost devoid of pebbles, with its peaty base exposed. This year the wreckage had been covered more and it made our search difficult. Marine life soon covers everything and to a pair of new divers every plant and animal is full of wonder and interest. Pollack swam passed leisurely, and occasionally a shoal of sand eels would dash by pursued by real or imagined predators. Large spider crabs spent their time slowly picking their way over the rocks and extricating their long limbs from around tangling bits of kelp. The occasional wrasse would swim up to us, give us a quizzical look, and then paddle away when it had decided we didn't represent any source of food. The dappled sunlight shone down through the water and caused the numerous pebbles to glint in the sun, a kaleidoscope of mineral shapes and colours.

Martin and Robert were like a pair of spaniel puppies, eagerly searching and examining every nook and cranny, enjoying every moment of their new-found world. Our air exhausted, we surfaced and climbed aboard the inflatable. Robert held out his hand. "Look what I found," he said, "just lying there on the surface of the sand" (Plate 3). It was a small brass padlock, seemingly hand made. It was rather delicate and pretty and it appeared to be quite old. Martin and I had both seen sherds of pottery. It seemed likely that these artifacts and the iron plates had indeed come from a wrecked ship.

We returned back to base and went out in the afternoon to hunt for some scallops which we were to have for supper. In the evening Martin and Robert went to get the air cylinders recharged while I prepared the meal. After supper we discussed the morning's dive. Could the site be worth a more intensive search? We decided it could.

A glance at a map of south western Britain will show that Devon has an extensive coastline, much of which is rocky and precipitous. Atlantic ocean waves striking against the cliffs erode the land away. The pieces that get dislodged vary in size from huge boulders through to tiny particles, these latter being carried by currents and wave action forming pocket beaches remote from their site of formation. If these lie undisturbed for long enough, these in turn may become different rocks (known as metamorphic, ie later-form). Such is the nature of much of Start Point – formed around four hundred million years ago of mica bearing schists.

Add to this the hard and soft parts of plants and animals and a range of burrowing and encrusting forms and you will see a considerable variety of conditions exist for ship remains to settle into. In addition the calcareous secretions of various organisms cement particles

Plate 3
"Look what I found" said Robert, "just lying there on the surface of the sand".

together and often, in the presence of pieces of iron, the rusting process causes solid lumps to form. Collectively these are know as concretion.

It is not my intention to write about the geology of Start Point, but to indicate the variety of conditions and difficulties in both finding, and once found, recovering maritime artifacts.

The conditions under which a ship sinks largely determines the fate of her remains. She may sink slowly in deep water or be violently destroyed in contact with land. The gradual disintegration of metals and wood vary according to several factors:

1 wave action
2 water
3 oxygen
4 light
5 marine organisms (including divers)
6 mechanical attrition

If the disintegration occurs slowly then a ship *may* be in an almost a similar state to that when it sank; the whole thing in a time capsule. This includes the presence and positioning of non-fixed items aboard the ship.

Sometimes parts of a ship may be preserved and other parts completely eroded. Two examples of wooden warships serve to illustrate the point. The *Wasa*, a Swedish vessel sunk in

1628 in Stockholm harbour on her maiden voyage. She sank into soft mud which almost completely covered her. The conditions prevented the decay of the wood but allowed thousands of the iron pins holding her hull together to corrode away. These had to be replaced by wooden ones before the *Wasa* could be recovered.

Nearer home, the 1545 wreck of King Henry VIII's warship *Mary Rose* sank on her side with the port side exposed above the sea bed (where it was subjected to centuries of anchors, trawls and the like being dragged over it and the exposure to the activities of biological decay). The buried starboard side survived under the Solent mud. This half ship was raised in 1982 and is now on display in Portsmouth where she was built nearly five centuries ago, together with thousands of artifacts and remains from her hull.

If a ship is wrecked having been driven ashore by the wind, then she may be smashed to pieces in a matter of a few hours. The physical disintegration would, of course, apply to components of, and objects contained within, the body of the ship. Thus pieces of wreckage and parts of the shore would be in turmoil and thrown randomly about. The order and natural assemblage of items would be vigorously disturbed. This chaos would be repeated over the years with succeeding storms. Having said that, it may be that a group of objects in close geographical position on a wreck-site may indicate a part of the ship not otherwise identifiable. For example, in a ship like the one we were researching, pieces of hull with portholes suggest places where people might look out, that is officers' quarters at the stern, not amidships; cargo is not interested in views. In our case we found various navigational instruments, the chronometer, a revolver and hand-cuffs all in the same area. They would expect to be in the care of the ship's captain, so it was reasonable to assume we were excavating in the area of his cabin.

It is doubtful if anyone with an untrained eye would recognise the shipwreck for what it was in our site because she was so broken up. Scattered remains were covered by rocks of various sizes but mostly shingle, sand and mud. In areas of some protection from what little current there was, the bottom was muddy. In areas where the cliff rock had broken up there were patches of sparkling schist often mingled with sand. The fine overburden ranged in depth from several inches to several feet. Scattered around were odd bits of iron and boulders up to the size of a car.

At the time I had no experience of searching the sea bed for artifacts, so we just dug into the soft material with our hands, wafting away the fine overburden which very soon covered everything in the vicinity. It was easy to create an artificial current and remove layers of fine material, but the concreted stuff required a totally different technique. Using a small club hammer the concretion was hit as gently as required to break up some fragments. These were then wafted clear and the 'new' surface examined to see what had been exposed, if anything. Any object appearing was gently teased from the surrounding material by using a fine chisel, a stiff brush (which had to be anchored between brushing to stop it floating away) or even teasing with a gloved finger. Larger objects in big pieces of concretion were dug out using a hammer and chisel. Frequently artifacts had to be wrapped in wet sacks for treatment back at home, more of this later. In the areas where the overburden and fragments of the ship had fused together to form concretion, the excavation was infinitely more difficult. I have sometimes used the simile of a road worker dropping something from his pocket when making a road, and many years later someone with a hammer and chisel trying to find it by haphazardly chiselling away here and there. There is just no more accurate way, the whole affair is very 'hit or miss'. Sometimes, when we found one thing, we would find several, rather like a seam of coal in a mine. More often, however, we would find nothing at all.

Plate 4 and 5
Robert 'wafting' and the result of excavations to a depth of approximately two feet. Note pieces of coal buried amongst the rocks – part of the Dryad's *cargo.*

Chapter Two

IDENTIFICATION

The following morning we were back on site, this time anchoring on top of those elusive plates.

After some time we had excavated a hole about a foot deep and a yard across. We discovered some frames and a piece of ironwork, together with lumps of concretion and pieces of heavily corroded iron. Robert, who had been swimming around the area of our excavation, came over and gesticulated for Martin and me to follow. He had found a large piece of plate which turned out to be part of the starboard side of the ship towards the stern, bearing a porthole. I thought this would be a good souvenir for Robert as a memento of one of his first 'proper' dives. We followed the line of the hull and sure enough, six feet away was another porthole, which I removed for Martin. I was confident that the next one would be for me, but all we found was a series of holes where they had been. I had to wait a number of years before

Plate 6 and 7
The recovery sites of the first two portholes.

I came across another, this time buried deep in concretion, just where it had been wrenched off as the force of the water on that fateful night had torn apart the hull, throwing pieces of the ship all over the place.

The padlock and the porthole Robert had found signalled the start of a series of finds which he came up with, which made us think he was blessed with some sixth sense for locating artifacts. He soon came up with a pair of navigator's dividers, and a battered .38 calibre bullet. In the next few days we recovered some of the sherds, a few items of cutlery, an ornate brass stair tread, fragments of what appeared to be a large bronze bowl and a splendid little brass dolphin. Because of the nature of our finds we thought it was likely that the area we were working was somewhere near the captain's quarters, so we nicknamed the area of the finds 'Captain's Cabin Gulley'. It came to pass we were correct in our assumption and eight years later I was to find the revolver which would have fired that bullet. (Gallery no. 60).

Merchant ships' captains in the nineteenth century often carried a revolver on board ship in order to have the ultimate sanction over trouble makers in the crew (and this was frequently the case). The gun was usually provided by the ship's owners "to enable the captain to ensure the safety and security of the owner's property". Handcuffs were also used in order to restrain obstreperous sailors, and eventually we did find a pair of these too. More of this in Chapter 10.

As captains were in charge of finances aboard ship, there was the possibility of finding specie: in those days gold coins were used instead of paper money. Having intrinsic value they were more readily acceptable in foreign lands. In any case the Bank of England did not issue pound notes between 1821 and 1928.

The thought of real treasure spurred us on, but in spite of the fact we dug down to the bare hull, systematically clearing a section at a time, very little else was recovered. I did manage to locate three coat hangers on which successive ship's captains may have hung their coats over the years, and a few copper nails from the wrecked ship's boats. Robert found a large piece of glass to fit his porthole, alas broken.

It is amazing how sometimes an innocent 'throw away' remark in conversation can prove to be very useful. I referred above to calling our excavation site "Captain's Cabin Gulley". Some years later I was talking with Alex Hurst – author of a number of books on square-riggers and who served on several including the renowned "*Moshulu*". We were discussing some of my finds at the wrecksite whose identity was causing problems and Mr Hurst remarked "ordinary fittings (such as coat hooks, etc.) in brass would probably be from the aft end of the ship (the officers' quarters), since had they been fitted in the fo'c'sle they would have been pinched". What did I say about Captain's Cabin Gulley?

All too soon we had to return to our respective jobs and there was no opportunity to dive again on the wreck that year.

Thus began the search, enquiries and research which became almost a religion (although some would say an obsession!). My quest must be similar to being passionately fond of jig-saw puzzles, yet having to find the pieces before starting to assemble the picture.

One minor detail was to stall my research for over eight years – I did not know the identity of the wreck. Bearing in mind the state of the remains, there was no basic structure to go on. The only thing I was reasonably confident of was the fact 'my' ship was not a steamer. Having dived many wrecks I knew one of the last things to disintegrate were boilers and engines. There was no sign of these or any associated machinery, so I was left with the conclusion she must have been an iron sailing ship. If only I could find something that would confirm or deny my suspicions. Quite often a shipwreck may be identified by a name or company crest on a fragment of pottery. Even though I had now recovered thousands of sherds, none had given me the slightest clue as to her identity. This in itself suggested that the ship was not a naval vessel, nor a passenger carrier whose crockery was often marked. Few of the fragments recovered show a similarity of pattern, so it was likely that she was a merchant vessel, with each member of the crew supplying his own crockery.

The fact that she was an iron ship indicated that she was probably built between 1860 and 1880, since before that date the majority of ships were still made of wood but by 1880 steel had largely superseded iron as a shipbuilding material. Iron may be recognised after a long period of immersion by its very grainy nature, the fabric rotting in a series of lines or ridges, whereas steel is more amorphous. This still didn't identify the ship of course, but it reduced the possibilities from many to just a few thousand. During their voyages round the world many were wrecked, but which one was 'mine'?

Living and working more than 200 miles away meant that the number of times I could visit the wreck was limited, not only by the availability of time, but also money, since petrol and hotel costs represented quite a bit out of my monthly budget. In addition the rough weather in late autumn, winter and early spring meant that perhaps six months would pass before I was able to dive again. Many is the time I travelled down to South Devon to be confronted by rough weather and heavy surf on the beach stirring Start Bay into something resembling oxtail soup.

Due to personal circumstances I did little diving in the next two or three years and unfortunately lost contact with Martin and Robert, who had both got married and moved away from their original addresses. Kathy, too, had married and gone to live in the Channel Islands. Thus new people were required to join the diving team when I recommenced operations. One day I was talking to a couple of friends in my diving club and explained the situation to them, and suggested that they might like to help with the project, emphasising that my interest was archaeological; systematically excavating the remains, plotting the position of any artifact found and conserving them as best I could. The one thing I hoped for was a find that would enable me to identify the wreck, and therefore possibly purchase her. I explained that I wanted to keep all the artifacts found in one place in order to avoid 'diluting' them and thus making it difficult to reconstruct the ship once her identity was known. This was agreed, but unfortunately one of the pair, when he started to find objects, insisted on keeping the more interesting items as souvenirs. He would not even let me take away some artifacts to photograph. Needless to say he did not dive on the wreck again.

At this time, of course, there was nothing I could do to stop the plundering of the wreck, and I do know of at least four diving groups who have removed artifacts. Just as some people become maniacs when they get behind the steering wheel of a motor car, so there are those who, having donned diving gear, must plunder and destroy wrecks just to raise to the surface some piece of non-ferrous souvenir which often finds itself gathering dust and cobwebs in the corner of a shed before being thrown away in the dustbin. I know for a fact this was the fate of part of the brass binnacle base. I dread to think of what else may have been removed and discarded in a similar fashion. Recovery without conservation is vandalism.

Part of the long frustration of not knowing the name of 'my' ship was, of course, the fact I could not set about buying or claiming an interest in her, since I didn't know who or what she was.

In my attempts to identify the wreck, I searched libraries for books on wrecks of the South Devon coast. I visited several museums in the area and searched in vain for clues. Local fishermen could only remember their grandfathers speaking of 'wrecks' around the Point.

Local publicans were intrigued and some amused by my requests for information. I borrowed all the books I could on local history, and asked in many local newsagents and bookshops if there were any records of details of wrecks. I always drew a blank.

I was careful not to talk to other divers about my find, to avoid them plundering for souvenirs, or worse still, scrap. In any case, how can you complete a jig-saw puzzle when someone keeps stealing the pieces? One bookshop owner suggested I tried the local newspaper archives. Well, they were very interested and helpful, but where do you start looking when you are not sure what you are looking for? I was, however, slowly gathering a short list of six or seven ships, but none of them seemed to fit precisely.

The *Lizzie Ellen* had gone ashore on rocks near Hallsands during the blizzard of March 1891 but she was a schooner of 73 tons; too small, and in any case made of wood. Even though it was highly improbable, I did use the name *Lizzie Ellen* as a sort of code name in the early days. The *Marana* was an iron ship of 1692 tons, but she was a steamer whose wrecking is well documented, having been watched by the Start Point lighthouse keeper's wife. The ship's remains are just to the south of the point against the Blackstone Rock, with her bow section a few hundred yards away towards Pear Tree Point – nowhere near my wreck, but you never know.

The *Spirit of the Ocean* was making heavy weather of a voyage from London, bound for Nova Scotia in March 1866. She was a barque of 578 tons and her master was trying to take her clear of Prawle Point, but the current and the so'therly gale carried her towards Start Point. The captain then decided to deliberately run her ashore in a little cove to the west of the Point, but she struck a rock some distance from the cove and broke up. Some parts of her hull were blown ashore, perhaps some of them had drifted round the corner?

The *Sandsend*, a 642 ton iron steam collier, seemed a likely candidate at first as she was wrecked close to Start Point, but a steamer would have boilers and an engine. Some pieces of wreckage bearing the works *Nymph of T . . .* were washed ashore near Hallsands in 1891 after some lights had been seen in the bay. As her name was incomplete it was impossible to find out more.

The *Lunesdale*, a 141 ton schooner was another possibility, but she was wrecked close to Beesands so it was unlikely that any of her remains would have drifted that far south and in any event she was wooden hulled.

The *Dryad*, an iron barque of 1035 tons seemed a distinct possibility, but one book I read spoke of an attempted rescue of a *Dryad* crew member in which local coastguards went down to a beach. The nearest beach is almost a mile away, so it seemed as thought the wreck couldn't have been the *Dryad*. Her cargo was coal and at the time I had seen no sign of any coal, again pointing away from her true identity.

Many ships have been wrecked along that piece of coast – indeed five vessels perished in one night but exactly which one was 'my' wreck was a tease which was to be resolved in a spectacular way one warm August afternoon.

The eighth of August 1982 dawned a lovely summer's day. The air and the sea were still, with pleasant 'seaweedy' smells in our nostrils as we loaded the inflatable. The water was warm as it seeped into our wet-suits. Our dives today were going to be good!

We arrived on site a little earlier than usual, and after securing the anchor close to where we were working, we began to dig again through concretion, moving any small boulders as they became loose. My log book reads "Chiselled and hammered for ages, nothing much found. Went to move what I thought was a grey stone and found it to be ductile. Dug around it and soon discovered it was a sounding lead". It took me another hour and a half to free it.

As it turned out to be the first and best of those recovered (see Gallery 38). Unfortunately a rather nice penknife was lying right alongside the lead and this was damaged during the chiselling. Artifacts buried and hidden from view are always in danger of being damaged, no matter how careful you are. There is no alternative to the hammering and chiselling process under the circumstances in which we were working, and I suppose I have been lucky in not damaging more.

I was very pleased with my find as I had been told that sounding leads were sometimes found with old shipwrecks, but this was the first I had found. It was carefully wrapped in a wet sack to be cleaned and conserved later at home.

The break for lunch (as always) included refills for the cylinders and, after a light snack and a short sun-bathe to warm bodies and digest the meal, we were away again. Whenever possible I like to return to the same work site I have just left, so with the sand and silt settled I can now see more clearly and search for any tiny fragments I might have missed in the gloom. The particular area I was in (between two frames of the ship's side) had been most productive and there was more to come. Now about 18 inches down in the overburden and concretion I found a brass peg spanner (see Gallery 21). I continued down towards the iron plates but found nothing more. I was getting low on air and a little chilly when I cast my eyes slightly to the right along the remains of a piece of cemented decking. One of the stones looked too regular to be natural so I moved in for a closer look. The greyish rounded mass did look interesting and I gave it a gentle tap with the hammer. Pieces of concretion fell off and I could see the glint of a brassy object beneath. My heart beat a little faster because, as I examined it, I could see what looked like lettering on the piece. I gave it a few more taps. More concretion fell away, and there was no doubt that it was lettering. I could clearly see the letters DR and below the top part of a W. My mind went over the possibilities. Of course! This was the brass cover over the opening in the deck where she took on freshwater, and what I was looking at was part of the words DRINKING WATER. It could just be that the peg spanner I found earlier was made to undo this cover.

By this time I was almost out of air. I had another full cylinder in the boat above and in a few minutes I was back on the bottom again gently chiselling round the edge of the brass. I had to proceed carefully because I was convinced that a large copper or lead pipe led away beneath towards the water tanks. It was around five o'clock by this time and the sun had swung round so that the cliffs of Start Point threw the wreck site into shadow but I could still see to work by. My find seemed to have warmed the water considerably! I had had a productive day and life felt pretty good. Here I was busy with another artifact and another piece for my jigsaw.

All of a sudden a stream of bubbles began to rise from behind the brass plate. (This often happens when an artifact becomes loose from its concretion and it releases trapped gases). I put my fingers over the plate and much to my surprise I lifted it straight up. It was not attached to anything and on turning it over I saw it was concave and domed. There was no sign of a pipe or anything else it could have been attached to. I turned it back over in my hand. Some five inches across, I laid it in my left hand and tapped the concretion with the hammer handle as, whatever it was, I didn't want to do it any damage. More flakes and pieces fell away. I stopped tapping and had another look. I just could not believe my eyes. My mouth spread into a huge grin; my face creased with smiles my mask began to leak. It didn't matter. My whole body tingled as though the blood in my veins had turned to champagne. What I had in my hand now confirmed my suspicions. After eight long years of searching, wondering and not knowing, I now knew. The object I held was the steering wheel boss, clearly engraved

"DRYAD LIVERPOOL"! Amazing though it seems now, I never even gave its true identity a thought; I was so convinced it was the drinking water inlet. The 'W' I had seen was the top part of 'IV' of Liverpool and the 'DR' of course being the first two letters of the ship's name.

I can honestly say that find gave me the biggest buzz of my life. I swam immediately over to my companion who took the photograph reproduced in Plate 8.

We surfaced and headed back for base. Once ashore I set about removing any further loose concretion before placing my find in fresh water. I imagined that that night someone would steal the car and my treasure with it, so I am not ashamed to admit I slept that night with the steering wheel boss by my pillow. It was still there in the morning so I knew it wasn't just a dream! Needless to say anything I found in the remaining two days of my trip would be an anti climax. I found absolutely nothing.

Over the next few weeks I considered the possibility of buying the remains, but I realised this would be a difficult task. There were just two groups who would be in a position to sell, the owners or insurers. The risk of loss around the time of the *Dryad* was great. Many owners

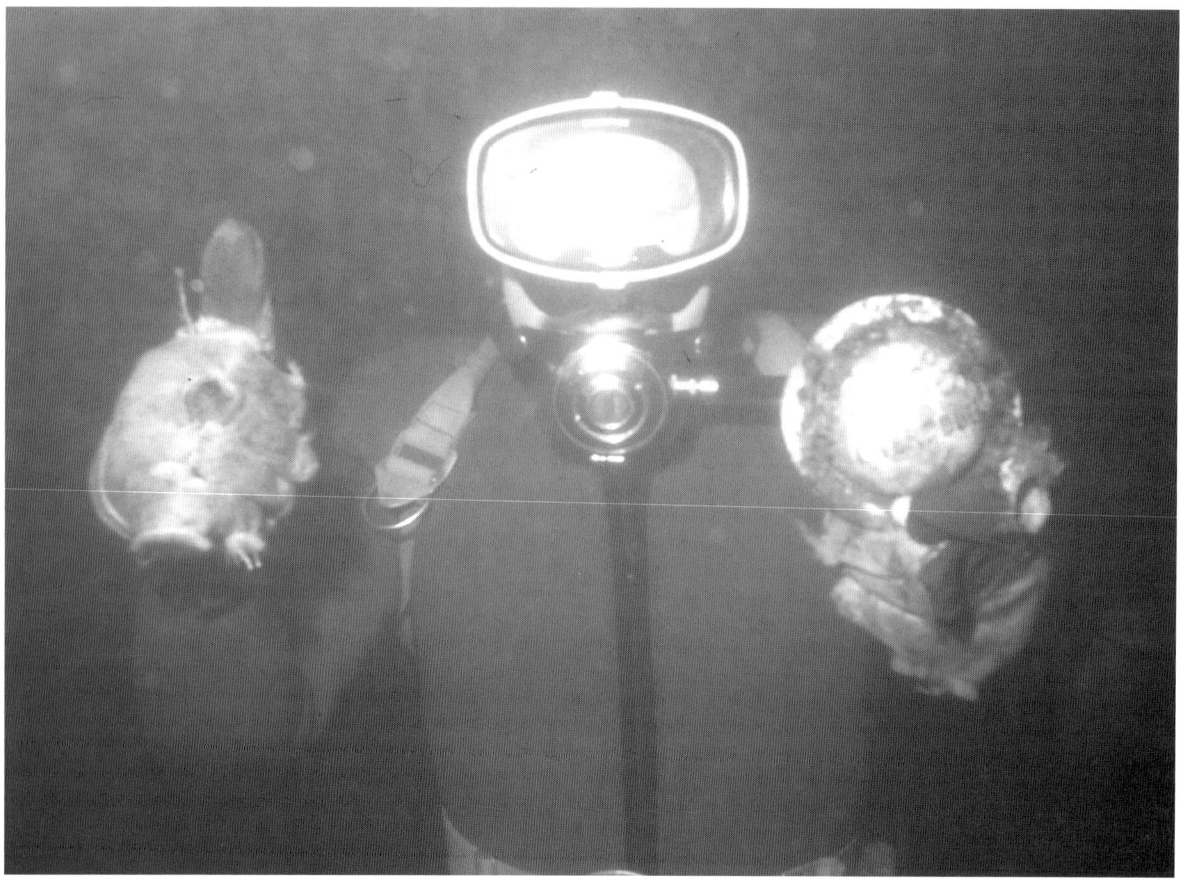

Plate 8
This photograph records the moment just after the recovery of the steering wheel boss from the wreck. Note the author's shredded gloves and happy state.

did not insure their vessels as the premiums would have been so high they preferred to take the risk themselves. I have been unable to trace any suggestion of insurance for the *Dryad* and the Salvage Association had no records of her. As for buying her from the owners, they would all be long dead. I had to settle for the 'status quo', that is salvor in possession.

Plate 4
The boss now showing the true identity of the wreck.

Chapter Three

RESEARCH – THE EARLY DAYS

Now I knew for certain the identity of my wreck, I could start researching her history. The National Maritime Museum in Greenwich was an obvious first step but they had disappointingly little information, just a few general references in Lloyds Shipping Index giving her measurements, confirming she was an iron full rigged ship and giving the name of her master at the time. I had earlier discovered that she was built in Liverpool in 1874 by T Royden & Sons and this was confirmed, together with the name and address of her owners. I enquired whether they had a photograph of her amongst their huge collection, but they hadn't.

I now knew, of course, that the *Dryad* was a Liverpool registered ship, and it would seem likely that someone somewhere in the great Merseyside metropolis had at least a few snippets of information useful to me. After a few preliminary enquiries I wrote to the County Museum. They were sympathetic and gave me what little information they had. This however simply duplicated what I already knew. One of the things I had enquired about was a crew list. They said they didn't have one and remarked that it was unlikely the crew list still survived, but I might try the Public Records Office at Kew. Now it so happened that this was only half an hour's car trip from where I lived. I thought the Public Records Office would only contain things like births, deaths and marriages registers and boring old government papers but nevertheless it was worth a try. I phoned them for further details. "Sorry, but we are closed for redecoration but you are welcome to visit us next month".

After a tantalising wait I arrived at Kew. I must say I was most impressed. Security is necessarily tight and after completion of the formalities I was allowed upstairs. People who work in such places are wonderful; extremely helpful and endlessly patient with folk such as myself who ask them obscure questions all day long. After being shown how to look up the indices to the records I wanted, they warned me that the records were very incomplete, and in any case only a 10% representative selection were held in this country. It appeared that so much material had accumulated since records began that any institution world-wide which would agree to house them could have them, subject to researchers having indirect access to the information. The Memorial University of Newfoundland in Canada now have most of the records. My initial excitement at the possibility of finding anything of interest vanished as I scanned the computer screen for the group numbers which were in this country and those which were abroad. I wondered at the enormous quantity of ships, and was rather dismayed since the number involved considerably lengthened the odds against my finding anything about 'my' ship. It seemed as though Richard Larn's warning about very little documentation surviving was about to be proved. My hopes were then slightly raised by the display indicating that the range of shipping records which included the *Dryad's* number were not in Newfoundland.

This meant that they were either missing or in the Kew collection. I ordered up the appropriate group of records and was eventually summoned to the counter and given a large, heavy cardboard box, the lid being tied down with faded pink ribbon. I took it back to my allotted seat and unwrapped the box. Hundreds of faded, dusty sheets of paper, parchment and the like spilled onto the table. They were roughly in alphabetical order, or so I thought, and I quickly sifted down to the 'D's. No *Dryad.* A great disappointment. Oh well, it was worth a try. Now I was here, I thought, I might just carry on and look at some of the material. Details of voyages, crews, problems, agreements, food, casualties all unfolded before my eyes. I was suddenly aware of details of a ship whose name I forget but it did begin with an 'A'. A cursory flick through several inches of the remaining documents showed that some of the material was not in alphabetical order, so there was still an outside chance that what I was seeking might be there. Hope faded as I carefully examined every sheet. I was within a few sheets of the bottom when suddenly, dog eared and blackened at the edges, there was what I was searching for. It was the *Dryad's* Agreement & Account of Crew, duly signed and dated by the master, Captain William Thomas, 25th February 1891. Also included were copies of the apprentices' indentures and some correspondence about exactly who was lost in the tragedy. What a piece of luck! My previous disappointment turned to joy as I busily copied as many details as I could. I now had a complete list of the crew, their ages, the amount of basic food rations that were allowed, where they were born and how much they were paid.

I really felt as though I was on my way. 'My' wreck began to take on a new perspective and I felt as though I could identify with the ship in a new way imagining all the exotic places she visited. Like most people, I suppose I had a romantic image of life aboard, jolly sailors sailing the seven seas, always with calm blue waters and a gentle breeze filling the snow white sails. The truth was far removed from this idealised world, with very sparse accommodation for the crew, who often had to turn to in the middle of a pitch black night in order to climb frozen rigging to furl sails against a screaming gale. The mountainous seas tossed the ship all over the place seemingly in an attempt to catapult the crew out of their lofty perches. If they made it safely back to the deck, those lucky ones not on watch would have no means of drying clothes or keeping warm. They had no chance to wander along to a modern galley and get a hot appetising meal. They were lucky to get a piece of bread. I felt sad that having endured such hardship the crew of the *Dryad* should be rewarded by being smashed into eternity against the rocks of Start Point. "Vessel wrecked, supposed drowned" – the relentless black ink spelt it out time and time again against the name of each crew member on the list. Was this to be their final epitaph? In some way I felt uncomfortable and strangely guilty that my enjoyment of diving on a wreck should have been bought at such a high price. I decided then and there that I would owe it to the memory of both the ship and her crew that the dusty sheets in the Public Record Office would not be the final words in the saga of the *Dryad.*

One day on a visit to the National Maritime Museum at Greenwich, I was thumbing through the books for sale in the shop area. I always do this, not only out of general interest, but to search the indices for anything related to the *Dryad.* In the references section of some pamphlet, the details of which I forget, there was listed "Thomas Royden & Sons,

Shipbuilders, 1818–1893". It was written by the grandson of Thomas Royden, Sir Ernest B Royden. The book was a must as far as I was concerned for it was, of course, about the builders of the *Dryad*. Frantic enquiries on my part produced a blank as no bookshop or library seemed to have heard of it. This was hardly surprising as, I found out later, it had been a private publication. I related the problem to the librarian at the London College where I worked. He was most helpful (as always) and made a lot of enquiries on my behalf. I was surprised to learn that the British Lending Library did not have a copy. However, a couple of weeks after this disappointment Norman told me he had located a copy in a North of England Polytechnic library and it was on it's way.

The book made brief but very interesting reading, giving some details of each of the 262 ships that the firm had built, namely the size, dimensions, type, year built and principal and some subsequent owners. One paragraph made very depressing reading from my point of view however, since Sir Ernest had written:

> ". . . a fire that occurred at the ship yard in 1879 resulted in the destruction of the office records, and when the business was closed in 1893 no records were preserved".

Years later, when I acquired a copy of the book for myself, I was very happy to see a covering letter stuck into the front of the book written by Sir Ernest to someone to whom he had presented the book, in which he repeated again his feelings:

> "As you will see it was most unfortunate that no records were left by my father when he closed the business".

I would like to be associated with that sentiment. It seemed likely therefore that I should never see the plans of my ship, or any photographs of her.

As a regular reader of the magazine Country Life I had often been struck by the number of correspondents making enquiries about lost pictures, genealogy, old buildings, etc, and more often than not the enquirer obtained some helpful information from fellow readers. It occurred to me that if information was forthcoming on paintings and buildings, then why not ships? My letter, when published, produced three replies.

The first was from a librarian who kindly pointed me in the direction of Richard Larn's book on Devon shipwrecks (which I already had on my bookshelf) stating there was a reference to the *Dryad* therein. The other two letters were really something special. To my great surprise and huge delight, I received a letter from a Mrs Mary Jenkins, who turned out to be none other than the great grand-daughter of the *Dryad's* captain, William Thomas, who lost his life in the wreck. The other letter was equally pleasing since it was from a Mrs Nancy Batten whose great grandfather was Thomas Royden, who built the *Dryad*! To hear from these two ladies was extremely fortunate and I made arrangements to visit them, tell them about my work so far and, of course, to ask many questions.

Mrs Batten, a charming elderly lady, could not help a great deal since, as she explained to me, even though a lot of the company records had been destroyed, her father (Sir Ernest Royden) had a considerable collection of archival material connected with his ancestor's shipbuilding firm in his Liverpool office at the beginning of the Second World War. Sir Ernest had to travel to London for a few days on business, and whilst he was away one of his employees was seduced by War Office propaganda into handing over all the papers to go for pulping! Mrs Batten told me her father was "furious". I would imagine that would be something of an understatement, and something I was not too happy about either.

Mrs Jenkins was able to supply me with a certain amount of information about the *Dryad*, mostly anecdotal of course, about the time her great grandfather had been the ship's captain. She also had three photographs, one of the ship and two of her crew. We cannot date these exactly or say where they were taken with certainty, but they must have been taken sometime between 1887 and 1891 as Captain Thomas is featured.

Following my initial contact letter and several long phone calls, I travelled to Pembrokeshire one weekend to meet Captain Thomas's descendants. Mary Jenkins and her family made me most welcome. We had a sort of *Dryad* party on the Saturday evening, me meeting the family and they gazing in disbelief at some of the artifacts from the seabed. I was also able to see and examine the sepia photographs. Mary had earlier sent me copies of these but they were no substitute for the real thing. Mary's young nieces naturally also wanted to look and my heart was in my mouth as eager young hands, covered in the remnants of a recently devoured cream cake, reached out for the priceless pictures. My best diplomacy and the intervention of their mother saved them and the day.

Mary told me that her grandmother Margaret had been the captain's only child and she was 16 years old when her father was drowned. Margaret had idolised her father and was naturally devastated by his untimely death. She had kept all his letters and some other papers, including some exercise books with his navigational calculations in them. These items had been kept by the family in an old chest which survived Margaret Thomas when she died in 1963 aged 89 years. There was no reason for Mr and Mrs Jenkins to take special care of the old letters and they were stored in an out building. In the fullness of time the roof leaked and water seeped into the chest. You may imagine the effect. When the disaster was discovered relatively few letters and papers were intact and these were scattered in various boxes and drawers and largely forgotten until I came on the scene. Mary and her brother have dug deep and so far found ten letters. Mary said if only she had known that in years ahead I would materialise, much greater care would have been taken. Alas, with hindsight, it is all too easy for any of us to be wise after the event. Nevertheless the letters which have survived make interesting and moving reading. They do give us a glimpse of life at sea in the late nineteenth century and the conditions under which Captain Thomas and his crew laboured. One of the first things Mary ever told me was how proud her great grandfather was of his ship and this comes through in his letters. (See Chapter 7).

One item belonging to Margaret Thomas which still survives is a hand muff made from the skin of an albatross, which was injured and despatched by Captain Thomas when the *Dryad* was in the South Atlantic in 1889. (Gallery 54) An old sailor's superstition is that if you harm an albatross then you will suffer a shipwreck. I will leave it up to you, dear reader, to judge whether the superstition is proved. Sometimes sea birds were shot on long voyages to provide some relief from salted meats in the diet, and a small calibre rifle was used for this purpose. One day I found 12 .22 bullets buried deep in the sand, lying in a small depression in a rock, and my mind wandered back to the albatross muff. Could these bullets have been the same batch from which was selected the fatal shot? (Gallery 36).

Mary told me how she came to read my letter in Country Life in the first place. Apparently one day she and her husband Haydn had been given some copies of the magazine to pass on to a friend. Haydn told me that on the Sunday morning he should have been in church but he was feeling a little lazy and decided not to go. He was just flicking through one of the magazines in an idle moment when his eye caught the headline on the 'Letters' page

"Iron Sailing Ship". He thought to himself "Mary's great grandfather sailed on one of those", and read on. He said he could not believe the rest of it because it was **the** one he sailed on! He told me he called out to his wife and ran to show her the letter. The rest, as they say, is history.

Another useful coincidence with regard to the research occurred one day when I was at college. A short course had been arranged on the use of a piece of electronic equipment and an expert from the manufacturer came to give a talk. I happened to sit at the same table at lunch as the demonstrator, and in the course of conversation she mentioned she and her husband were going to Melbourne, Australia, for a holiday in a week or two. Now it so happened that one of the best runs the *Dryad* ever achieved was between New York and Melbourne, a total of 84 days. Not only was this good for the *Dryad* but was sufficiently fast to warrant a newspaper article about it in the Melbourne Argus. I knew this because Captain Thomas had mentioned it in a letter home. I was keen to see this and asked the demonstrator if she could enquire if the newspaper was still printed. Amazingly she replied that one of her husband's favourite hobbies was looking up old records and she promised she would see what she could do.

A number of weeks went by and I received through the post not only a photocopy of the article, but a couple of small advertisements from the same paper concerning the *Dryad*, her cargo and crew. How kind, thank you Pauline. (See Chapter 5).

One day I happened to be visiting a friend in Las Vegas, USA. It was a relatively short flight to San Francisco and I had wanted to visit the National Maritime Museum there for some time, and also to meet some of the people with whom I had been in correspondence over a photograph and possible other records of the *Dryad* in the archives at the Fort Mason Centre.

San Francisco has a number of historic ships moored along Fishermans Wharf, including the *Balclutha*, a British built full rigged ship of similar build and size to the *Dryad*. Although some 12 years younger than the *Dryad*, there were bound to be similarities in her structure and fittings and a visit was a must. It was a still, misty morning as I waited for the entrance booth to open up so I could go aboard. I used the time studying the ship from the outside, imagining her pitching and rolling in the turbulent seas around Cape Horn and mentally transporting myself back 100 years. (Plate 11).

Once on board I was not disappointed. In the pantry for example, there was a brass gimballed candle lamp identical to the one I had found on the *Dryad* five months earlier. It showed me that the mounting collar for the lamp chimney (which I then discovered was a sliding fitting) had seized in the wrong position in my lamp and had stuck there due to the accumulation of concretion inside the collar. This had been difficult to remove, so I had left the collar in its wrong position in my ignorance. Discussing this with the conservationists at Fort Mason lead me to discover another kinder way of removing concretion using a chemical I was not familiar with. (For those interested a 10% solution of sodium sesquicarbonate = 22.6 grams per litre of distilled water – causes calcareous concretion to slowly dissolve). There were many other similarities of fittings on the *Balclutha*, and it was easy to imagine I was on the *Dryad*.

I examined the binnacle base with its three brass dolphins, very similar to the fragments recovered from the *Dryad*, and the steering mechanism was similar. I observed how some of the artifacts I had raised from the *Dryad* must have fitted into the structure, for example the hand-rail ball by the stairs and doorway. The fiddle rail on the sideboard in the captain's quarters was almost identical with the one that Robert had located two years previously under

Plate 10

The Dryad *at anchor, possibly the Thames. Note she has now been cut back to a barque rig, in contrast to plate 12, in which she is still as launched, that is a as a full rigged ship.*

Courtesy: Thomas Family, Pembrokeshire.

Plate 11
The Balclutha. *This magnificent restored British built ship lies alongside Pier 43 in San Francisco. I enjoyed every moment of my visit on board which became a sort of 'virtual'* Dryad, *some items being identical to those found on my wreck.*

Plate 12

The Dryad *at anchor in San Francisco. The* Dryad *visited San Francisco on three occasions, each time under the command of Captain John Evans. This photograph will have been taken in the summer of 1876 or 1881, or the very early part of 1880. Note that she is still a full rigged ship, and that her sails have been unbent from the lowest three yards, possibly for repair. the main yard has been braced round (the rest of the yards squared) in order to facilitate cargo handling – a common practice then. It is likely that the* Dryad *had only recently been towed into her position here as her tow-rope is still loosely coiled on the staboard forward ship's boat. The galley chimney is clearly visible, just aft of the foremast, between the two boats. When a ship was in harbour, as here, the crew usually had a little more time to themselves and were able to catch up on domestic chores like laundry, which can be seen hanging up to dry forward of the deck house in which the majority of the crew lived.*

Photo: Courtesy of National Maritime Museum, San Francisco.

a large plate of iron on the wreck. I had noted to my surprise, that parts of the *Dryad's* fiddle rail supports appeared to be chromium plated, and that those on the *Balclutha* certainly were, so this could have been standard practice on some ships since it would have reduced a little the amount of brass work to be cleaned and polished.

After several hours I returned to the twentieth century and mused over the sad fate of thousands of these magnificent ships. What a pity there are only a 'handful' left in the world today for us and future generations to enjoy. It appals me to think how often we just let priceless history become rotten, or destroy it for scrap.

In 1875 for example, the year the *Dryad* first started her career, a total of 56,505 sailing ships were registered by the world's major seafaring nations; 19,709 in England alone. Not all of them were of the size of the *Dryad* of course; the world wide average tonnage being 263 tons for that year. Nevertheless it gives some idea of the number of beautiful vessels that have failed to survive.

Also in San Francisco was a restored example of one of the Liberty ships, one of over 2,700 which were built on a production line basis in the USA. to bring much needed supplies to war-torn Britain in the 1940's. I mention this because one of these ships lies wrecked not very far from Start Point and is probably Britain's most dived upon shipwreck – the *James Eagon Layne.*

Whilst I was in Fort Mason I treated myself to another copy of the photograph of the *Dryad* in San Francisco Bay (see Plate 12), this time an enlargement for hanging on the wall at home. As always the staff were very helpful, and in spite of my arriving at Fort Mason without prior notice I had my photo in a matter of hours, delivered the following morning to a place much more convenient for collection as far as I was concerned, as I was due to leave for England at midday. It was nice to meet and talk with people who, until then, had just been signatures at the bottom of replies to some of my endless enquiry letters. We searched for possible further information on the *Dryad* but unfortunately nothing came to light. She had covered her tracks well. Clutching my large photograph I headed back to England.

Amongst the mountain of mail awaiting me on my arrival home was a packet from the Memorial University of Newfoundland containing twelve crew lists and agreements over the years, giving details of various happenings while the *Dryad* was in foreign parts. I was surprised to read how many of the crew deserted. I knew this was a commonplace occurrence with crimps enticing crews away, but who would want to desert the *Dryad*? Further details of some of these incidents will appear later on.

Chapter Four

THE BUILDERS AND THE BUILDING

Liverpool's growth and prosperity was closely linked to the fact that the city was built on the estuary of the river Mersey. Thus trade with other parts of the world could be readily conducted through shipping. The development of Liverpool as a port was enhanced in the very early eighteenth century when Liverpool Corporation decided to build an enclosed maritime dock, said to be in an attempt to overcome the vagaries of the Mersey tides, currents and sandbanks. The dock handled a variety of imports and exports, and was to become the world's first mercantile dock system with deep water berths and lock gates to retain the water so that ships could remain afloat at all states of the tide.

By the end of the eighteenth century it was larger and much more sophisticated than any of its potential competitors. As a result the relatively small town grew into a bustling metropolis which, by the time the *Dryad* was launched in 1874, had a population of 493,405.

Not only was Liverpool one of the most important trading ports in Britain, but she naturally attracted a fair number of shipbuilders. For a variety of reasons the dock system was constantly being reconstructed and enlarged. Not only were the docks sometimes in need of repair and improvement, but changing cargoes and their storage needed new buildings. Relatively inexpensive imports such as timber could be stored on the dock-side, but the increasing importation of valuable commodities, such as tobacco, needed secure warehouses and these naturally required land. Perhaps the most important reason for the expansion and enlargement of the docks was to accommodate the increase in size of the ships themselves.

The shipyards required to be close to the river to facilitate launching, and the continuous digging and alterations of the dock system could not have endeared the corporation to the tenant shipbuilders, especially as reclamation of the Mersey river bank, on which the builders built their ships, was often part of the leasing agreement. Many shipbuilders gave up the struggle, and by the mid nineteenth century more than a dozen Liverpool shipyards had closed. The situation of any shipbuilding firm was precarious, with no security of tenure. The Dock Trustees (a committee appointed by the corporation) charged high rents for the sites, and issued only short term leases. If the trustees required the shipyard sites for any other purpose the builders could be asked to leave with little notice given and no compensation.

Roydens were fortunate in being able to stay at their Baffin Street works until 1893 when the inevitable happened and the site was required for the building of new docks. Maybe Sir

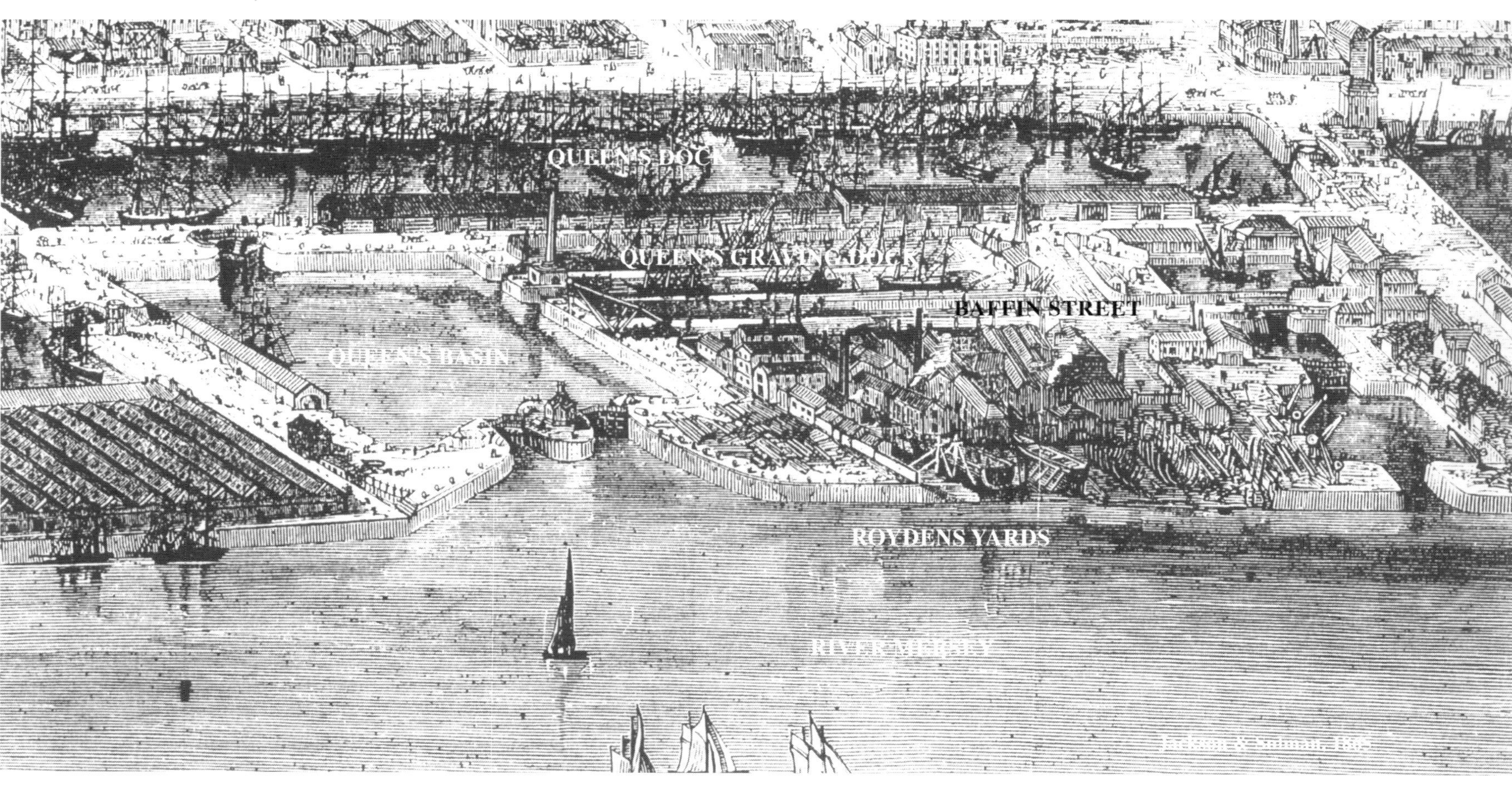

Fig 1

This engraving is part of an astonishing view drawn from a balloon tethered above the River Mersey. The artists Jackson and Sulman, employed telescopes as well as photographs: although photography was in use by 1865 there was no satisfactory method of halftone reproduction until the 1890's. This was fortunate, as wood engravings, unlike photographs, made the finest detail distinguishable, on the far horizon as well as the foreground. The view here shows Royden's Yards and Offices and associated docks, and several ships in various stages of construction.

Reproduction by courtesy of Scouse Press, Liverpool.

Thomas Bland Royden's eminence in local politics had something to do with the relatively long life of the yard.

One anonymous writer in the biographical sketches in 'Our Shipping Headlights' put it thus:

> "It required no prophet to read aright the signs of the times, and to see that Liverpool, as a ship-building centre, was doomed. Sooner or later the Dock Board would require – as they have now done [1900] – the site of the yard for dock extension."

The same author also pays tribute to the quality of the workmanship of the company by writing:

> ".... In its palmy (sic.) days the celebrated Royden yard would compare for quantity and quality of work turned out with the best".

In the 75 years the firm was in business a total of 262 ships were built.

The *Dryad* was laid down in Roydens' Baffin Street yard as ship no 164 in the late spring of 1874. She was launched on Saturday 7th November the same year. She was one of a number of iron ships built by Roydens with their reputation of excellent workmanship and materials, and graceful lines.

The firm of Thomas Royden was founded in 1818, originally as a partnership between Thomas Royden and a James Ward, firstly as a firm of ship repairers, who in the early 1820s turned their attention to ship building. Their first ship was a wooden schooner, the *Rhyland Castle*, of 84 tons gross which was launched in 1823. The following year two larger ships were built, the *Mersey* of 328 tons and the *Rocket* of 237 tons. 1824 also saw the dissolving of the partnership due to the ill health of James Ward.

In 1825 the firm suffered a huge setback in the form of a fire, which not only gutted the buildings and store, but destroyed two ships on the blocks, one of them almost completed. The estimated cost of the damage was £25,000, a considerable sum of money in those days. In 1828 a John Watson of Chester was taken into partnership, but the firm was known only as Roydens. The partnership was dissolved some seven years later and from this time on only members of the Royden family were involved with the firm, right through to the cessation of business in 1893.

One of the biggest changes to occur during the lifetime of the firm was the development of iron as a shipbuilding material, compared with the traditional wood. At first iron was quite expensive, but it got cheaper as the British iron industry expanded. Within a few years it was cheaper than wood, and as far as the Liverpool shipbuilders were concerned they had also exhausted local supplies of suitable timber. Thomas Royden had to travel as far as Shropshire in order to find oak of a quality and shape good enough to go into a Royden ship. He and he alone was the only person he considered had sufficient expertise to select the correct trees.

I do not propose to examine here the development of iron merchant sailing vessels. There are a number of books on the subject by authors far better qualified than I, but a few background details may be of interest in fitting the *Dryad* into the general picture. In the early days of development of ocean going merchant vessels, ship builders and designers relied far more on experience than theoretical technical know-how. Once a good design had been arrived at, it was frequently copied time and time again. Thus a present day researcher who is in the know can often recognise ships from a particular yard by their characteristic line. By looking at Royden ships from a similar period, it is possible to reconstruct some of the features of the *Dryad* not visible in the photographs of her – in much the same way as I suppose one might recognise the work of a particular artist.

Sometimes the design of ships was regulated by parliament. This was once done in an attempt to prevent the escape of fast sailing craft from the clutches of his Majesty's cutters out to catch illegal slave traders or smugglers. Speed was sometimes important for commercial reasons, for example the fruit schooners. These craft (usually smaller than 200 tons) had perishable cargoes aboard and needed to get to their destinations quickly. In the case of cargoes such as coal, jute, nitrates, etc, bulk carriage was of greater importance, and many ships were built with slow but commodious hulls. These apparent conflicts in ship design were gradually refined so that it was possible to have a craft that could carry substantial amounts of cargo at a fairly fast pace. Competition between different companies to be able to advertise the fastest passage was keen, and many ships' masters needed little encouragement to press their ships along. The ultimate pinnacle was reached in the development of the clipper ships with their grain races and the fact that the first consignment of the new season's tea to arrive often commanded the highest price.

It will be seen therefore, that as the nineteenth century progressed, so ship design became more specialised. The development of iron as a shipbuilding material was an important step forward in the middle of the century, and a couple of decades later this began to be superseded by steel. The use of steel coincided with the development of steam power, which rang the death knell for sailing ships. The *Dryad* may therefore be considered to be typical of a sailing merchantman at her zenith.

Iron ships were much stronger than the old wooden ones and less prone to leakage, since iron rivets holding plates together did not 'work' to the same extent wooden planks did. Iron plates could be much larger than planks of wood, so the number of joints and therefore potential sources of leaks were less. Iron ships were lighter than their wooden counterparts size for size and could carry a correspondingly larger cargo. Many ship owners realised their advantages and ordered iron ships from the early 1860s onwards. However, Thomas Royden was a traditionalist and said he would retire from the firm if ships were ever built of iron. They were, and he retired in 1862 at the age of 70 years. His elder son Thomas Bland Royden then took over the firm and the first iron ship was the *Silvia* (1401 tons) launched in 1863. Three years later Thomas Royden's younger son Joseph joined as a partner and from then on the firm was known as Thomas Royden and Sons. Perhaps the old man was rather set in his ways and preferred to let his two sons develop the new material and its associated technology.

Compared with centuries of building wooden ships and the experience and expertise gained therefrom, the construction of iron vessels was of course an innovation and a few problems arose at first. The iron played havoc with the navigation, since it affected the ships' compasses, but once compensating mechanisms had been developed to overcome compass deviation this was no longer a problem. It has been suggested that an inaccurate compass was responsible for the *Dryad's* demise, since during the hurricane the helmsman was steering by dead reckoning, being unable to see due to the blinding snow; he thus sailed into Start Point instead of clearing it out to sea. However, I have been unable to find any documentary evidence to support this.

Wood was still used extensively in the construction of some parts of the ship, notably the deck and deck houses. Originally masts and spars were made of wood, but this later changed to iron as the technology developed to enable lighter, yet stronger, units to be used. At the time of her building, the *Dryad* was a modern ship, even having galvanised iron wire shrouds. According to her final survey she was supplied with wire standing rigging, and hemp running rigging, "sufficient in size and quality". The *Dryad's* decks were made from four inch thick yellow pine, and there are still fragments of the decking buried under the mud, sand and rocks of Start Bay. (see Plate 13).

Plate 13
Remains of decking and a dead eye.

Some of it is still in remarkably good condition, and I used to imagine back to the days when the crew were down on their hands and knees holystoning the deck to keep it spick and span. I find there is always a great sense of identification with the crew when I am diving on the ship. It is sometimes difficult to realise that they are not there with you. It is easy to imagine silent faces peering at you, watching you work.

One of my favourite anecdotes, passed on to me by Captain Thomas's great granddaughter, was that the captain was so proud of his command and her deck that the ship's carpenter was instructed to inspect the footwear of all visitors on board *Dryad* to make sure that they had no hobnails or similar likely to damage the woodwork. The carpenter was told to remove any such offending items before the visitors were allowed to walk the deck!

Reference has already been made to the fact that iron was a relatively new ship building material and judging from contemporary and modern comments upon the *Dryad* it seems as though Roydens put it to good use in constructing this ship. There is no doubt that the *Dryad* was a very fine looking vessel and that she had, and for that matter still has, many admirers. Captain Thomas was very impressed and wrote home after his first trip out from England in his new charge "*I must say that the Dryad is a* ***noble*** *ship and will go past everything, and I am very pleased with her.*" A captain's pride in his ship no doubt, but there is evidence to show that she did make some fast voyages. She was of very similar build to another Royden ship, the celebrated *Merioneth,* which recorded the fastest ever passage from Britain (Cardiff) to San Francisco in 96 days.

In spite of the impressive results produced by iron ships, it would seem that Lloyds Register Committee still regarded the material with an element of suspicion and used to 'watch points' fairly closely with regard to build quality. No doubt this was brought about by the frequency of dismasting reported in the case of a number of large iron sailing ships; often during maiden voyages, in the years 1873–74. Lloyds Register of Shipping issued a special report about the problem on 2nd December 1874, less than four weeks after the launch of the *Dryad* and this report was printed a fortnight later in The Times. So it was no surprise at all to learn that Lloyds questioned Thomas Royden & Sons about the strength of the masts, spars and rigging of the *Dryad* at the time. I realise, of course, that the National Maritime Museum in Greenwich was not specifically built for the benefit of me and 'my' ship, and that it is not always possible for them to find things that they have hidden in the archives. They may not even know they are there. Although I have made a number of general requests to various sections and departments over the years, no plans or photographs had so far emerged. They do not have the resources to go through everything in the entire complex just on the off-chance that something *Dryad* will be unearthed. Naturally they can only look for specifically asked for items.

The manner in which the correspondence came to my notice was another piece of remarkable luck and good fortune for me when, in the spring of 1990, I was in correspondence with the Museum over clarification of a detail in the Lloyds first entry report – the final survey on the new ship – when much to my amazement and delight, a very helpful gentleman in the manuscripts section made a surprising discovery. A young chap had been seconded from the Australian Museum to Greenwich for a few months study and rummaging through some cupboards/drawers came across an old unlabelled brown envelope with some papers inside. Curiosity caused him to look further. He discovered some correspondence about the *Dryad's* masts and rigging, including a piece of yellowed oiled paper being a tracing of the rigging plan of 'my' ship. The tracing was naturally old, faded and rather dirty. A photocopy proved unreadable but the Museum's photographic department worked wonders and I now had an acceptably good plan. As far as I am aware, it is the only one in existence, since all Thomas Royden's records had been destroyed by the fire at the yard in 1879, some five years after the *Dryad's* launch.

It turned out to be the most expensive photograph I have ever bought, but I considered it well worthwhile. It is reproduced on Fig 2.

The first of the letters accompanying the rigging plan (which bore no heading) came from the secretary of the London Committee (HQ) of Lloyds Register to their local surveyor at Liverpool.

> "*Sailing ship Dryad.*
> *It is submitted that this ship is eligible to be classed 100 A as examined. As howevere the masts appear to be deficient in strength as compared with the committee's suggestions, it is considered desirable that more detailed information should be supplied, setting forth whether*

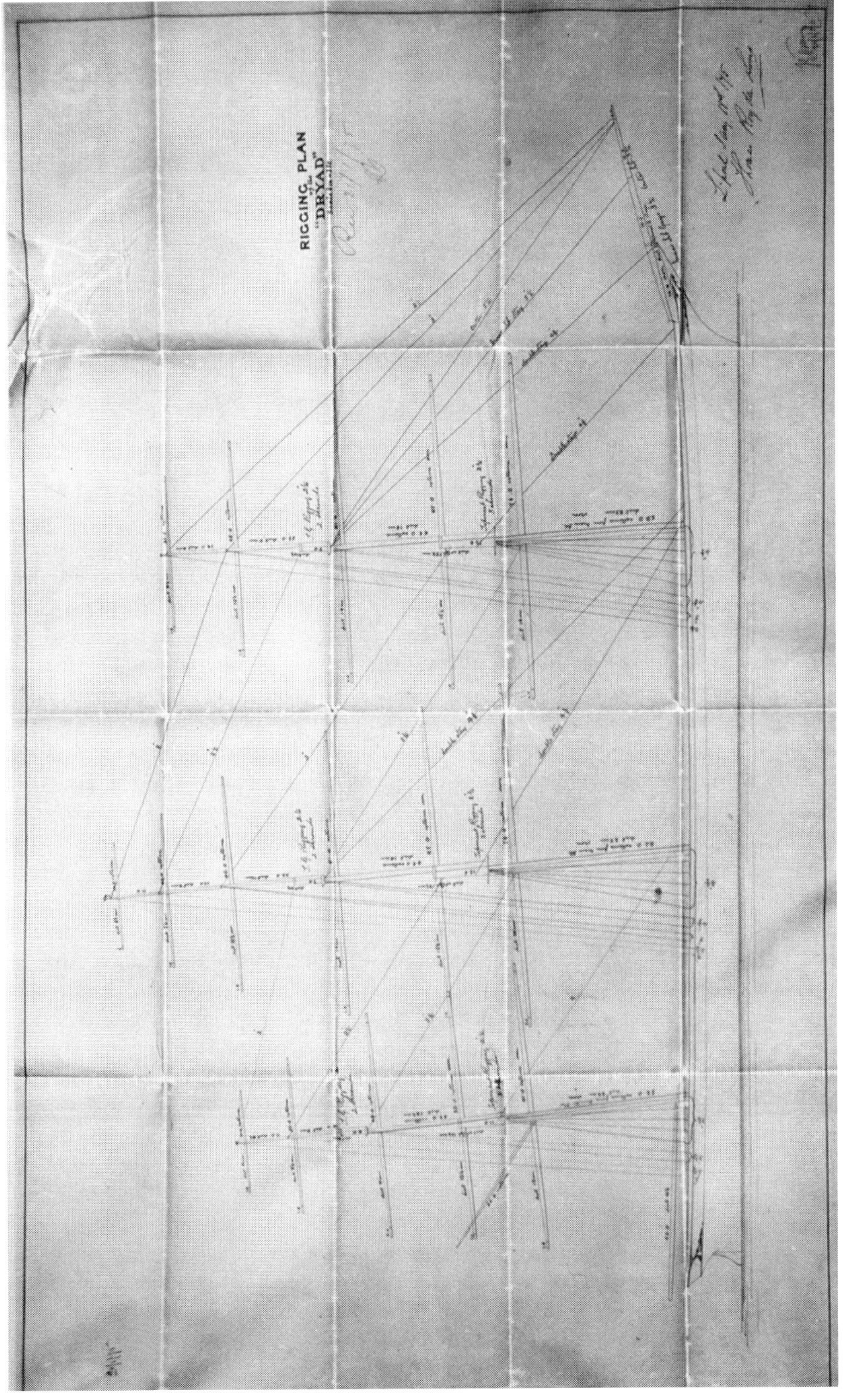

Fig 2
Copyright The National Maritime Museum, London.

a diaphragm plate has been fitted in the Bowsprit, and the mast plating doubled at the wedging. Also the ? of the treble riveting should be given and the diameters of the principal yards; and in view of the smallness of the masts, the size and number of the Shrouds and Stays should be given for the information of the Committee; together with sketches of masts and spars with detailed particulars."

B.W.
11/1/1875

The reply:

LLOYDS REGISTER OF BRITISH & FOREIGN SHIPPING.
B. Waymouth, Esqr., *LIVERPOOL 20th January 1875*
London, E.C.

"Sir,
Referring to your letter of 14th instant, I herewith enclose a letter of this day's date from Mr Wheeler, with a Rigging plan which Messrs. Royden & Sons have been so good as to furnish, giving the fuller detailed particulars desired of the Masting & Sparring of the new iron ship Dryad. Report No 24,444 from which it is thought it will be seen that the masts cannot be considered, as seems to have supposed they were, deficient in strength as compared with the Committee's suggestions, unless it be the Mizen Mast in respect to which the latter seem to make no distinction in size and scantlings, as governed by length, from those for Main and Fore masts.

I shall be obliged by your sending me, as early as may be practicable, a copy of the Register Book for Messrs. Rose, Thomson & Co., of this Town; whose names I have had the pleasure to add to the list of Subscribers here and which accordingly be so good as to direct to be inserted in due course in the published lists.

I am, Sir,
Your obedient servant,
R.E. Mudge."

The third letter, dated 20th January 1875, was from Mr E C Wheeler (who was the *Dryad's* surveyor and author of the report) and gives great detail of the construction and measurements of the masts and bowsprit, and measurements of the rigging (see later in this chapter). Each part or section has its description and, where relevant, small sketches to show the construction of the mast or yard. Alongside the dimensions given is another list in red ink and a different hand, headed 'Rule'. It would seem this has been marked in by someone from the Committee, comparing the individual measurements. Those of the *Dryad* are usually bigger, although where smaller the difference is insignificant. Mr Wheeler ends his letter:

"It will I think be seen from the foregoing detailed report that the Fore and Mainmasts and also the bowsprit are not below the suggested Rules, and as regards the Mizen such as usual below (both in scantlings and diameter) that of the Fore and Main masts.

The builders (Messrs Royden) have kindly furnished me with a tracing of the spar and rigging draft which I beg to enclose for the Committee's guidance.

I remain Sir

Your Obedient Servant

E.C. Wheeler.

It will be seen that Lloyds were necessarily cautious in granting their 'seal of approval' to a ship. The granting of a Lloyds' classification certificate was very important from the builder's point of view. As Sir Thomas Bland Royden himself put it, when giving an after dinner speech to celebrate the 50th anniversary of the re-organisation of Lloyds on 30th October 1884 held at Cannon Street Hotel: "*I venture to say that wherever a British ship goes, bearing the classification of Lloyds' Register, in whatsoever part of the world, she is accepted as being fit to carry any cargo offered.*"

It is interesting to note that the author of the first letter (11th January 1875) and initialled "B.W." was written by none other than Bernard Waymouth, who was at the time the secretary to Lloyds Register, having been their principal surveyor for two years prior to this. Waymouth will perhaps be best remembered for his designs for the fast sailing ships, in particular the celebrated tea clipper *Thermopylae*, which was involved with the famous *Cutty Sark* in the early 1870s as they raced across the world from China to Britain with the new season's tea. I have read somewhere that *Thermopylae* was the fastest sailing vessel of her type ever built.

As the old saying has it "It's an ill wind that blows no-one any good". Had it not been for the Lloyds Committee enquiry, the plan would never have been seen past the date of the fire in 1879 at Roydens which had destroyed all the records, and I would never have been able to examine it, nor include it in this book for that matter.

The *Dryad* was laid down sometime in early 1874 and was the last of eight ships built by Roydens that year. It is noteworthy that of these eight, four were steam ships for the recently established company of F Leyland & Co (ex Bibby Brothers) of Liverpool; so even at the time of her building the writing was on the wall for sailing ships.

Once the First Entry Report (survey of the ship by Lloyds) had been located in the National Maritime Museum, it proved to be a rich source of information about the ship. The iron from which the *Dryad* was supplied by Clough Hall & Co, Stockton Iron Works and Skearn Iron Works, although the last named company is listed in the official survey as being the type of iron used.

Her measurements were as follows:

Length 203.4 ft
Breadth 34.7 ft
Depth 21.25 ft.
Gross tonnage 1069.19
Nett tonnage 1035.27
Underdeck tonnage 997.38
Keel depth and thickness 9" x 2 3/8"
Stem depth and thickness 7½" x 2 3/8"
Stern post depth and thickness 7½" x 2¾"

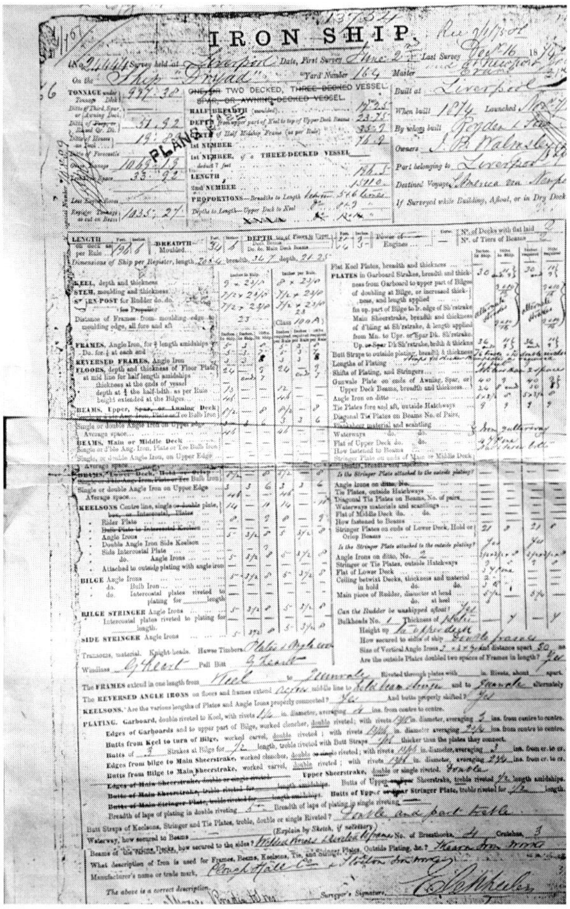

IRON SHIP.

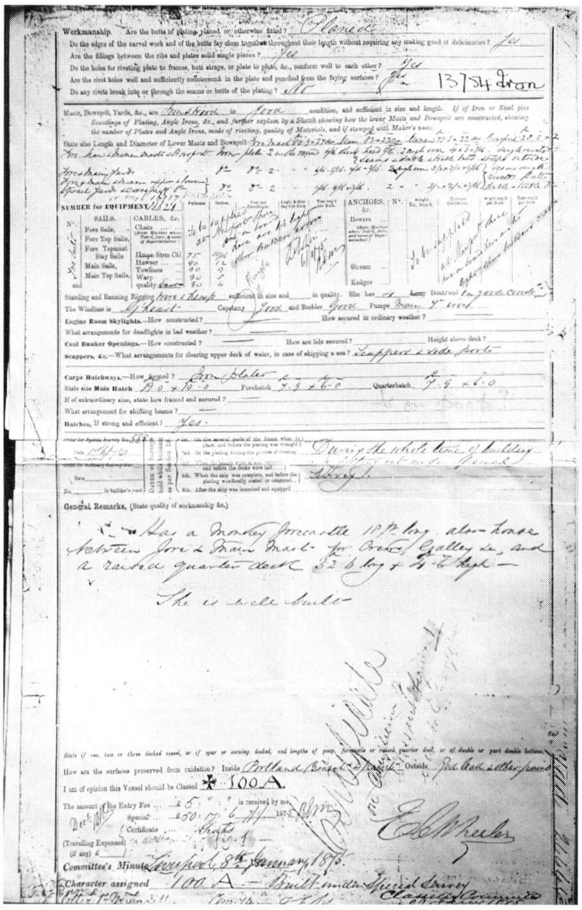

General Remarks, (State quality of workmanship &c.)

Has a monkey forecastle 18½ long, also house between fore & main mast for crew, galley &c, and a raised quarter deck 32 6 long & 4 6 high —

She is well built

I am of opinion this Vessel should be Classed ✠ 100 A.

Fig 3

First Entry Report Number 24,444. The final survey on the construction of the Dryad.
She is classified ✶ 100 A. Written across the base of the report are the words "she is well built".

Frames 5" x $3\frac{1}{2}$"
Distance between frames (edge to edge) 23"
Floor depth and thickness (for half length around mid line) 24" x $^{9}/_{16}$"
Upper and Lower Beams $8\frac{1}{2}$" x $\frac{1}{2}$"
Keelson 14" x $^{11}/_{16}$"
Rider plate 8" x $^{9}/_{16}$"

Masts and Yards

	Length	Diameter
Fore mast	80' 9"	27"
Main mast	83' 0"	27"
Mizzen mast	77' 8"	22"
Bowsprit	28' 8"	23"

Fore and Main yards	74' 0"	18"
Cross jack	61' 0"	15"
Fore and Main lower and Topsail yards	67' 0"	15½"
Mizzen lower and Topsail Yards	53' 0"	12¼"

The frames of her hull were built (two angle iron bars riveted together) and extended in one piece from keel to gunwale. Her plates were 11' in length by 30" wide for the garboard strake; 36" wide in the rest. She was clench built with 5' overlaps on each plate, double riveted together for the most part by 1³/16" rivets. The plates were planed to make sure the overlapping surfaces were smooth and free from nibs, spots, spelter, etc., which might otherwise create gaps and therefore leaks.

The deck beams were secured to the sides by means of welded knees, riveted to the frames. Decking was of yellow pine, 4" thick on the upper deck, 3" thick on the lower deck, and a 2" thick ceiling of the same material between decks. The timber being secured to the beams with nut and screw bolts.

The rudder had the mainpiece 5½" diameter at the head; and 3" diameter at the heel. It was designed to be unshipped at sea.

The *Dryad* had a single collision bulkhead built in ⁷/16" iron plate which extended right up to the upper deck.

Up in the bows there was a small monkey fo'c'sle 18' long for storage of some sundry items of ship's gear and possibly a pig sty and chicken coups; on its roof the windlass, capstans, bollards and the bell. Incorporated into the fo'c'sle unit was of course the chain locker, with its 90 fathoms of stud link chain. Aft, a raised quarter deck 52' 6" long and 4' 6" high carried the steering gear, binnacle, saloon skylight and access to the hold and senior crew members' quarters. By tradition the captain's quarters were on the starboard side of the ship, the mate's on the port side, and usually the saloon in the middle.

Between the fore and main masts a deck house rated at 19.89 tons housed both crew and galley. This may readily be seen in the two photographs of the ship (Plates 10 & 12). There were three cargo hatches, the main hatch being 19' 0" x 10' 0", and both the forehatch and quarterhatches measuring 7' 9" x 6' 0".

Dryad carried four boats, two carried on the deck house roof and two further aft on a special frame called the skids. Her main pumps for keeping the hold free of water were of iron, 7" in diameter, located just forward of the mainmast. She was, like most of her contemporaries, equipped with two sets of sails, the better set often being reserved for rough weather, the poorer set bent on in lighter airs.

One item I found rather curious in the First Entry report was that written across the space on the form to describe the size etc. of the chain and anchors: "*To be supplied at Newport those put on board here [Liverpool] are too light thro' Builder's error*". It was initialled R.E.M. (Mudge) and dated 6/1/1875. Although I have traced the crew agreement for that voyage, so far I have been unable to unearth anything about the anchors and chain themselves. It does seem rather strange that Roydens should have made such a mistake, especially when one considers that the *Dryad's* yard number was 164 and the builders should have learnt a bit by then.

Her initial survey was carried out on 2nd June 1872 but she was surveyed throughout her building and fitting out under special survey number 588, the order for which was dated 17th

June 1874, at a cost then of £50–17s–6d (£50.87½p). The last build survey was dated 16/12/1874. Following the anchor and chain debacle at Newport 21/1/1875, in spite of the problems, Lloyds finally awarded the *Dryad* the top classification of 100A, writing in the comments section of the First Entry Report "She is well built".

Whilst the *Dryad's* exterior surfaces were protected by red lead and other paints, the inside was cemented. Portland cement (mixed with sand) was frequently used to protect inner surfaces from corrosion and abrasion. In the early days when I first examined some of the decking and remnants of the bilges I mistook the cementing for a thin layer of concretion, but I soon realised this was far too regular and symmetrical to be a natural phenomenon, and that it had to have been applied by the hand of man. This was confirmed when I read the survey report and realised it was protection for the plates. The cement was made up into a cream like consistency and applied with brushes. It was said to be easier to apply than oil paint and had the additional advantage of adhering to damp plates, which paint would not. Also the alkaline nature of the cement reduced corrosion caused by the acidic nature of the bilge water, and further helped to guard against wear and tear on the plating and rivets caused by loose objects rolling about on the bottom with the action of the ship at sea.

I remember reading a long while ago about the celebrated Royden built (1875) *Merioneth* who sailed the fastest ever passage from Cardiff to San Francisco in 96 days. She, like the *Dryad*, was a flyer and part of the explanation for the speed was that her bottom was painted with a special glass smooth white enamel-like paint, which was manufactured by the Liverpool firm of J & W Wilsons & Co. This was said to slide through the water easily and resisted the adhesion and growth of fouling organisms. The *Merioneth's* bottom was said to be "like china" at the end of the record voyage by her mate George E. Stewart.

At first I dismissed the idea of the *Dryad* also being painted thus, as the two photographs I had seen showed her with a dark hull. However I consulted the microfilm records of local newspapers at the Cookworthy Museum in Kingsbridge which enabled me to search through all the snippets of information about the 1891 storm wrecks, and on several occasions I saw the *Dryad* referred to as having a brown and white hull, or being chocolate [brown] with a white bottom. Now, in both photographs (plates 10 and 12), the ship was fully laden, so a white bottom would be hidden beneath the water. Time to research my 'odds and ends' files, especially the numerous 'blow ups' of parts of the ship. Sure enough, at the bow and again at the stern and rudder top a clear white line is showing, just above the water. So the *Dryad* did have a white bottom after all! It is tempting to suggest it was that same special glasslike enamel used on the *Merioneth*. Both ships built within a few months of each other by the same yard to similar specification (although somewhat different sizes) strongly suggest it was.

If a comparison is made between plates 12 and 10 it will be noted that the rigging is different between the aft mast or mizzen mast in each. In Plate 12 the *Dryad* is ship rigged, in plate 10 she is barque rigged.

In a ship rig the sails carried by transverse spars are all square; in a barque rig the sails on the mizzen mast are not, but lie along the length of the vessel, i.e. are fore and aft. There is no doubt that she was built and launched as a full rigged ship but she had been converted to a barque by the late 1880s. Despite my efforts, I have been unable to trace when and where this conversion took place.

There were two possible reasons for the change; 1) reducing the cost of running the vessel, 2) a desire to improve her handling. In the first case square sail rigging all round took more crew to operate than the fore and aft rig of the barque. Thus fewer crew meant a smaller wage bill. Secondly, the *Dryad* may not have handled as well as she could. A curious comment made by Captain Thomas in one of his early letters home suggests this (see letter 3rd March 1887 from Valparaiso) in which he says that the *Dryad* had previously been "given a black name". He went on to deny this, saying that in his experience the "*Dryad* would go past everything". Perhaps as Commodore Captain of the Walmsley Fleet he was able to harness the potential of his ship to the best, more so than the earlier critics could do.

One item of the *Dryad's* structure which I found intriguing was the figurehead. It took me a long time to locate any information at all. All that might be gleaned from a close examination of the ship's photographs is that the figurehead was quite large and a pale colour overall.

The origin of figureheads apparently dates back to the very early pagan seafaring times when the head of a sacrificial animal was placed on the ship's bow in order to placate the gods and therefore ensure a safe passage. Later the head became symbolised, and on some ancient warships featured prominently to make the whole ship appear more fearsome. The ancient Egyptians painted eyes on the bows to enable the ship to 'see' where it was going. Much later, in the middle ages, British ships often featured heraldic beasts or symbols and later busts of heroes – either folk or naval. In the latter part of the 19th century, figureheads of female figures predominated.

Many maritime carvings including figureheads were anonymous but sometimes, if the carver was a well known local craftsman, details of his work were given in the local newspaper when the ship was launched. So I found myself in the British Newspaper Library at Colindale, reading through all 23 newspapers and periodicals published in Liverpool around the launch date of the *Dryad.* This was not an easy task. The printing was often small on faded and yellowing pages and the fact that reports were usually not headlined, meant every word had to be examined. In spite of the close scrutiny, no details emerged of the *Dryad's* figurehead. It is tempting to suggest that the figurehead was of a wood nymph, i.e. a dryad. As mentioned above, female figureheads were popular around the time of *Dryad's* building and the one on the bow of the *Dryad* could equally well have been a portrait of a member of the owner's family as was sometimes the case. I happened across an article which mentioned in passing that ship's registries in the various ports sometimes carried information on figureheads. Liverpool's Customs & Excise were helpful and partially successful in that they unearthed the description of a "demiwoman", so either of my two guesses could fit. However no more precise details have come to light.

I have not been able to determine why the *Dryad* was so called. "Dryad" is a generic name for a large class of inferior female divinities. Specifically, the name means a wood nymph, one that inhabits a tree. They are not immortal but extremely long lived. On the whole, dryads are kindly disposed towards mankind. There is a fungus called dryad's saddle (*Polyporus squamosus*) which bears a remarkable similarity in shape to the old fashioned farm tractor seat. I suppose a tree dwelling nymph may be forgiven for using a similar fungus as a seat!

One tale, told by Sir Ernest Royden in his book about the family business, bears repeating. It relates to the origin of its address, i.e. Baffin Street. Apparently, in the eighteenth century, before the erection of the shipyards there, Liverpool ships played an important role in the Greenland whale-oil industry. The oil, from whales caught in Baffin Bay, was brought to Liverpool in barrels which were unshipped by simply throwing them overboard, later to be run ashore and up the beach into holding tanks. Thus the connection is made between the site of origin, Baffin Bay, and site of delivery, later Baffin Street. As far as I am aware, *Dryad* was never involved in this sort of activity.

Plate 14
Bidston Lighthouse, built 1771 (rebuilt 1873).

Mrs Batten spoke to me about a number of paintings owned by her late father, Sir Ernest B Royden, some of which were reproduced in his privately published book "Thomas Royden & Sons, Shipbuilders 1818 – 1893". These depicted local scenes and ships. One of these illustrated the flagstaffs on the top of Bidston Hill on the Wirral peninsular (Plate 14). From the top of the hill ships bound for Liverpool could be observed approaching eastwards quite some time before they entered the mouth of the Mersey. Once identified, the ship owner's house flag was run up the mast, thus alerting the owner's agents in the port to the ship's imminent arrival.

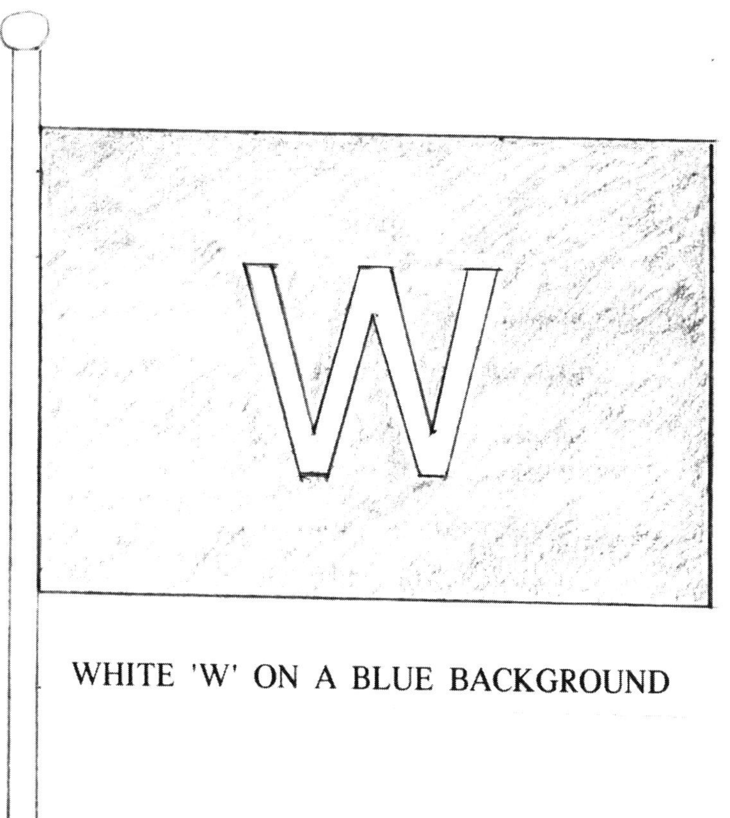

Fig 4
House Flag for sailing ships of J B Walmsley and Co, Liverpool.

This system of signalling was superseded in 1827 by a series of semaphore stations, which in turn were replaced some 30 years later by the electric telegraph. The association between Mersey shipping and Bidston was further enhanced in 1867 by the building of Bidston Observatory, set up to make observations and measurements of the stars and other meteorological events. Later work on tides was undertaken and continues to this day. One of the important pieces of research work at the observatory was to establish the exact latitude of Liverpool so that ships' chronometers could be accurately set. A series of very accurate clocks were set up and together with a system known as the "One o'clock gun" enabled ships' captains to set their chronometers accurately. Precise timing was of course vital when sun sightings were taken on board as part of the measurements necessary to calculate the position of a ship at sea.

DRYAD'S OWNERS

Traditionally the ownership of a vessel was split into 64 shares. A month after she was launched the *Dryad* was registered on 7th December 1874 with John Bankes Walmsley, Shipbroker of Liverpool, owning 64 shares. On 15th March 1875 he sold two shares to Thomas Archer Lowe, Commercial Traveller of Tranmere, two more to Henry Davidson, Master Mariner of Liverpool, three to Frances G. Wheeler, Spinster of Tranmere, four to George Ferris Sanders, Gentleman of Liverpool, two to Joseph Atkinson, Gentleman of Tranmere, and two to Thomas Simpson, Coal Merchant of Rock Ferry. On 16th March 1875 he sold another two to Francis Pitt, Master Mariner of Liverpool and on 20th of the month he sold two to Frederick Joseph Bartlett, Gentleman of Liverpool. On 3rd April 1875 he sold four shares to John Aitken of Rhyl and on the thirteenth of the same month he sold four to James Smith, Gentleman of Liverpool. On 15th October 1875 he sold two shares to George Whitfield Bullock, Shipowner of Manchester. On 24th July 1879 he also sold three shares to Henry Luke, Master Mariner of Liverpool. This seems to be the sum total of share transactions (32 all told) by Walmsley in the register. It would seem therefore that half of the 64 shares were split between J.B. Walmsley and the rest.

I am indebted to Mr Michael K. Stammers, Keeper of the Merseyside Maritime Museum for supplying me with the above details. He also informs me that there may be a continuation book/s in which further details of *Dryad's* ownership are given, but these were not available at the time of writing.

Chapter Five

VOYAGES

The first voyage (if it may be called such) was the run from Liverpool to Newport to rectify the problem of the chain and anchors. The *Dryad's* first captain, John Evans, was master for this trip and he was accompanied by 15 crew consisting of first and second mate, a steward, two apprentices (one only 14 years old) and ten able seamen described as riggers. They were engaged from 17th December 1874 "on the run from Liverpool to Newport", and it was "agreed that they shall remain on board for twenty four hours after the ship has arrived at Newport Spit, if not docked before". The riggers were to be paid £2–10s–0d "per run" which, considering they were discharged on 20th December 1874 and that the standard wage for seamen at that time was approximately £3 per month, they would seem to have been very well rewarded for their efforts. The crew agreement states simply "No grog allowed" and the details of the crew's rations during the voyage equally baldly put "As much as will be required".

Most people with even just a passing interest in ships and shipping will know that Lloyds of London publish a paper known as Lloyds List which details all movements of shipping world wide, amongst other maritime matters. I wrote to them seeking information on the *Dryad.* Poor devils, they must be fed up with receiving thousands of such letters every year. Their duplicated reply was short but to the point: ". . . to make these records more accessible to the public, the whole collection has been passed to the Guildhall Library . . . to whom you should now address your enquiry". I decided to go there in person. A newish building in the general area of the Guildhall in the City of London was soon located and following the regrettable, but necessary, security checks I was allowed inside. As I approached the librarian's desk I was pondering how to ask for over 17 years' worth of Daily Index to search through for anything *Dryad.* However I need not have worried as when I explained the problem to the ever helpful staff I was relieved to discover that there were reference indices to books collating the information I was seeking. I was given some tomes which listed ships alphabetically and arranged year by year. These enabled me to construct a list of detailed references to the *Dryad* entries.

Leaving aside difficulties like the fact that the index books were compiled in handwriting which was not always easy to read, and that 'my' *Dryad* was not the only one listed, I eventually came up with 193 references. All I had to do was look through approximately that number of Lloyds Lists of the appropriate dates and I would have my very own *Dryad* list. I started there and then but only managed to look up five or six before closing time. It may seem a long time but two and a half years elapsed before I managed to complete my list. Naturally I could only visit the library spasmodically and it was just not possible to do more than a few dates in a day. Not only the physical searching for the item but copying it down when found all took longer than I anticipated. Also sometimes there were delays in ordering up the bound volumes and, even though a lot of them are now on microfilm, sometimes one had to wait for a viewing screen to become vacant. It all helped to spin out the time involved in tracing the movements of 'my' vessel over the oceans and ports of the world in her 17¼ year life span. I reproduce them below. I have also included, where appropriate, extracts from newspapers and periodicals which give details of incidents and cargo listings.

HISTORY OF THE *DRYAD'S* TRAVELS; COMPILED PARTLY FROM LLOYD'S LIST 1875–1891

1874	Launched Liverpool 7th November 1874	
	18th December:	Sailed from Liverpool for Newport
1875	226th January:	Sailed from Newport for Talchahuano (Chile). (Evans master).
	Speakings:	2nd February 50N 13W by the *Astracan* (Allan master)
	Speakings:	21st February 5N 26W – no ref.
	Speakings:	1st March 4S 29W by the *Annie Fletcher* (Rae master).
	5th September:	Arrived in Liverpool (Evans master) from Tome (Chile)
	6th September:	"The *Lancashire* (ferry boat) and the *Dryad* from Tome were in collision in the river, last night; the former lost one funnel which fell on the saloon; the latter has little or no damage.

Extract from "The Daily Post" (Liverpool) Monday, September 6th, 1875.

A WOODSIDE FERRY IN COLLISION

"Last night an accident occurred in the river which might have been of a very serious character. The ferry steamer Lancashire, Captain Bloor, was crossing the river from Woodside, which she had left at 10.45, and was in the act of crossing the bows of a ship (the Dryad) which is anchored nearly opposite to the stage on the other side of the river, when the ferry boat was carried too near, and the bowsprit of the vessel knocked down the starboard funnel of the ferry boat. The ponderous mass crashed down on deck in the midst of a number of passengers, two of whom were severly injured, but not sufficiently to prevent their being conveyed to their homes. Others were slightly hurt. The Lancashire discharged her passengers and proceeded on her return voyage to Woodside, where she has since been laid up for repair".

	15th October	Sailed from Liverpool for Calcutta (Evans master)
	Speakings:	25th October 37N 12W by the *Hipparchus* (Hudson master)
	Speakings:	27th November 23S 23W by the *Vallejo* at Queenstown.
	Speakings:	20th December 10S 28W
1876	18th February:	Arrived in Calcutta from Liverpool (Evans master).
	19th April:	Sailed from Calcutta for San Francisco (Evans master).
	9th June:	Arrived Punta Arenas (Chile) from Calcutta (Evans master).
	29th July:	Arrived San Francisco from Calcutta (Evans master).
	13th September	Sailed from San Francisco for Liverpool (Evans master).
1877	14th January	Arrived Liverpool from San Francisco (Evans master).
	26th February	Sailed from Liverpool for Calcutta (Evans master).
	27th February	*Dryad* reported as arriving off Bardsey Island (N. Wales) on route Liverpool to Calcutta.
	Speakings	28th February 49N 12W by the *Salisbury*.
	Speakings	23rd March 4N 23W – no ref.
	3rd May	Arrived in Calcutta from Liverpool (Evans master)
	23rd July	Sailed from Calcutta for London (Evans master).
	6th November	Deal (S. England) passed en route Calcutta to London.
	7th November	Arrived Gravesend from Calcutta (Evans master).
1878	14th January	London Customs entry: cleared outwards for Calcutta (Evans master).
	18th January	Gravesend sailed for Calcutta (Evans master).
	24th January	St. Helen's Road arrived.
	26th January	Signalled off St. Catherines Point. (I.O.W.) *Dryad* bound for Calcutta from London.
	26th January	Bembridge Roads, I.O.W. Sailed for Calcutta.
	13th May	Arrived in Calcutta from London (Evans master).
	3rd December	Sailed from Calcutta for New York (Evans master).
1879	Speakings:	2nd February 23S 4E en route Calcutta to New York. All well.
	7th February	St. Helena – (S.E. Atlantic) sailed for New York.
	27th March	Arrived in New York from Calcutta (Evans master).
	13th May	Cleared for Sydney (NSW).
	16th May	Sailed from New York for Sydney (Evans master).
	Speakings:	1st June. No position quoted, but all well, by the *Vandalia*.
	Speakings:	5th June, 26N 33 w, steering SW – no ref.
	Speakings:	10th June, 13N 30W – no ref.
	Speakings:	15th June, 5N 27W by the *Cardigan Castle*.
	3rd September	Arrived at Sydney (N.S.W.) from New York (Evans master).

THE SYDNEY MORNING HERALD *Thursday, 4th September 1879*

Shipping

Arrivals – September 3

Dryad, ship, 1035 tons, Captain Evans, from New York 14th (sic) May.

Passengers – Messrs. Lockrey and Brown. Agents: R. Towns & Co.

Imports – September 3

Dryad, from New York:

9 cases waggons
600 cases sarsaparilla
46 packages shoe pegs
405 cases chairs
112 boxes axes
57 cases sewing machines
19 cases organs
48 boxes jars
3 cases cigarettes
96 boxes clocks
12 packages hardware
2500 cases Kerosene oil
680 oars
50 cases blacking
120 wood buckets and covers
5 boxes starch
480 washboards
50 boxes clothes pins
7 packages glassware
652 boxes scales
300 cases spirits of turpentine
21 cupboards
450 barrels resin
5 cases painkiller
21 pieces machinery
200 quarter barrels apples
10 cases books
100 pairs wheels
445 pieces and packages timber
150 tons coal
1828 packages

"The ship Dryad, from New York, brings a general cargo of American goods. She sailed on 14th May, with fine weather which continued through the N.E. Trades; crossed the Equator on the 22nd June, in longitude 20°W. and after experiencing moderate S.E. trades had W. and S.W. winds to the Cape of Good Hope, the meridian of which was crossed on the 22nd July, in 40°S; thence had moderate winds to longitude 70°E; made on the 9th August; between that date and the 18th had four successive hard gales, with a high sea; passed Cape Otway on the 27th August, and had fine weather on the coast."

	7th October	Sailed from Sydney for San Francisco (Evans master)
1880	? January	Arrived San Francisco from Sydney (Evans master) *"San Francisco. During a gale on 25th January the Alex McCullum (ship) commenced dragging, and in a short time was foul of the Dryad (British Ship). Some damage resulted and the vessels were drifting steadily towards Alcatraz, but two tugs went promptly to their assistance, when they were separated and moored into safe positions."*
	24th February	Cleared for Queenstown (Eire).
	28th February	Sailed from San Francisco for Queenstown (Evans master).
	29th June	Arrived Queenstown from San Francisco, carrying wheat.
	30th June	Sailed from Queenstown for Dublin.
	2nd July	Arrived in Dublin.
	4th August	Arrived in Liverpool from Dublin.
	28th August	Sailed from Liverpool for Calcutta (Evans master).
	Speakings:	1st September off Kinsale by the *Belfast*.
	Speakings:	No date. 46N 41 bound west (sic) by the *Heela*.
1881	6th January	Arrived in Calcutta from Liverpool.
	16th March	Sailed from Calcutta for San Francisco (Evans master).
	12th July	Arrived in San Francisco from Calcutta.
	29th August	Cleared for Liverpool.
	31st August	Sailed from San Francisco for Liverpool (Evans master).
	29th December	Arrived off Point Lynas.
	29th December	Arrived in Liverpool from San Francisco.

Cargo: *314 sacks of borax*
47 bales of cotton
1,000 cases of canned goods to sundry cosignees
550 cases of fruit
600 sacks, 520 ¼ bags, 1000 ½ bags flour
25,430 sacks of wheat Order

1882	8th February	Sailed from Liverpool for Valparaiso (Evans master)
	10th February	*Dryad* put in to Holyhead through stress of weather. (Fresh gale force 8) from SSW.
	19th February	'Sailed' from Holyhead (in tow).
	20th February	Sailed from Holyhead for Valparaiso (Evans master)
	Speakings:	22nd March 2N 27W – no ref.
	Speakings:	25th March 1S 29W – no ref.
	6th June	Arrived in Valparaiso from Liverpool (Evans master).
	10th June	Sailed to Caldera (Chile)
	15th June	Arrived in Caldera.
	14th July	Sailed from Caldera for Pisagua.
	21st August	Arrived in Pisagua from Caldera.
	4th October	Sailed from Pisagua for United Kingdom for orders (Evans master).
1883		Arrived at Queenstown from Pisagua for orders.
	18th January	Passed to sea past Roche's Point for Dunkirk (sic).
	26th January	Anchored off Deal (Pisagua for Dunkirk).
	1st February	Sailed from Deal.
	2nd February	In the roads of Dunkirk.
	28th February	Sailed from Dunkirk for Cardiff (Evans master).
	1st March	Dungeness – passed West 10.11 am.
	3rd March	Prawle Point (Devon) passed down 4.30 pm.
	5th March	Arrived in Penarth Roads, Cardiff.
	7th March	Arrived in Cardiff (Evans master).
	6th April	Sailed from Cardiff for Iquique (Chile) (Bradbridge master).
	Speakings:	26th April 5N 26W – by the *Star of Bengal*.
	30th June	Arrived at Iquique from Cardiff (Bradbridge master).
	13th October	Cleared for England from Iquique (Evans master).
	Speakings:	30 October 34S 83W – no ref.
1884	19th February	Arrived in Falmouth from Iquique with cargo of nitrate.
	25th February	Sailed from Falmouth for Bordeaux.
	26th February	Dover 11.34 am. "*The fishing smack Ernest of Lowestoft, Capps master, has been towed in here dismasted, by tug Cruiser (agreement 35) Captain reports having been run into at 5.0 o'clock this Morning, off Dungeness by the barque Dryad of Liverpool, from Iquique for Hamburg, which vessel proceeded without damage*".
	5th March	Cuxhaven (N. Germany) arrived from Iquique (Evans master)
	8th March	Arrived at Hamburg from Iquique.
	20th April	Sailed from Cuxhaven for Cardiff (Evans master).
	22nd April	Dover – passed east.

	23rd April	Prawle Point 3.00 pm *Dryad* passed down (for Cardiff).
	27th April	Arrived in Penarth Roads.
	3rd June	Sailed from Cardiff for Iquique (Evans master).
	4th June	Cleared for Iquique from Cardiff.
	Speakings:	1st July 12N 26W steering South – no ref.
	Speakings:	12th July 5S 31W, bound South – no ref.
	22nd August	Arrived at Stanley, Falkland Islands, with Captain Evans ill. "*Stanley, (F.I.) September 12th. The Dryad ship of Liverpool put in here August 22nd with master sick. She is still detained here; Captain Evans being too ill to be removed (sic) at present. (The Dryad is bound from Cardiff for Iquique).*
	19th September	Sailed from the Falkland Islands for Iquique (Evans master).
	28th October	Arrived in Iquique from Cardiff.
1885	21st January	Sailed from Iquique for Pisagua (Evans master).
	25th January	Arrived in Pisagua from Iquique.
	30th May	Arrived in Falmouth U.K. from Pisagua carrying nitrate (Evans master). Sailed from Falmouth for Hamburg (Evans master).
	11th June	Dungeness 12.00 noon. *Dryad* (barque) passed east.
	19th June	Arrived Hamburg from Pisagua (Evans master).
	24th August	Sailed from Hamburg for Sydney, Australia (Jenkins master).
	29th August	Sailed from Cuxhaven.
	1st September	Dover 8.00 am. *Dryad* (barque) passed West (Hamburg for Sydney).
	3rd September	Scilly 10.00 am. *Dryad* passed West Hamburg for Sydney.
	13th December	Arrived in Sydney from Hamburg (Jenkins master).

THE SYDNEY MORNING HERALD *Monday 14th December 1885*

Shipping

Arrivals – December 13

Dryad, barque, 1035 tons, Captain R Jenkins, from Hamburg August 29.

Agents: R. Elkan & Co.

Imports – December 13

Dryad, from Hamburg.
320 cases beer
10 cases spirits

301 cases furniture
84 bales 10 packages paper
10 cases toys
96 cases pianos
53 cases glassware
40 cases woodware
7488 barrels cement
15 cases methylated spirits
3 casks wood spirit
2 cases chinaware
50 cases bitters
50 cases rum
10 casks cordials
5 casks glucose
1 case art flowers
7 cases paintings
2 cases hardware
7 cases slates
6 cases basketware
6 cases musical goods
1 cask asphaltum
10 cases pot flour
3 cases concertinas
20 casks paint
2 cases cigars
59 cases balls
2300 cases schnapps
2 cases mouldings
2 cases crockeryware
1 trunk effects
1107 cases
30 packages

"Several years have elapsed since the Dryad, which arrived yesterday [December 13th] from Hamburg with a general cargo, last visited the port, but she does not look much the worse for wear since she was here. Captain R. Jenkins is in command, and reported that she sailed on August 29, and had light winds and fine weather till taking her departure from the Scilly Islands on September ? . Across the Bay of Biscay the weather was very squally, but after that, light winds and pleasant weather prevailed to the trades, which picked up in about 29°N, proved light and well from the eastward. They gave out in 6°N., and after two days of variables the S.E. trades were struck in about 4°N. Crossing the Equator on October 2, in 32.4W the Dryad had light winds down to 20°S, and variable weather thence for a few days. On October 14, when in 30.32S.,and 31°W, the Dryad was sailed by a heavy gale, lasting for about eight hours, during which the vessel was hove to. A high cross sea accompanied the storm and kept the decks constantly filled, but no damage was done. Steady winds and moderate weather followed to the Cape of Good Hope, the meridian of which was crossed in 40°S on October 31. Off the Cape the Dryad

had to cope with another heavy gale, the wind veering between S.W. and N.N.W., and bringing along another tremendous sea, but as before the vessel came through uninjured. The gale lasted for ? hours, and the ship had to be hove to during part of this time. The easting was made between the parallels of 40° and 43°, with winds veering generally between north and west, very seldom coming from the south and west. Cape Otway was sighted on the 8th instant and easterly winds followed for three days. A fine westerly breeze then sprang up, and lasted until the barque was abreast Gabo Island, whence southerly and easterly winds prevailed to port. The Dryad entered the Heads at half past ? yesterday morning, and anchored below Ganden Island."

	31st December	Melbourne. The ship *Dryad* from Hamburg at Sydney reports loosing several sails in a heavy gale from the north.
1886	14th January	Arrived at Newcastle (N.S.W) from Sydney (Jenkins master).
	10th February	Sailed from Newcastle for Portland, Oregon, U.S.A. (Jenkins master).
	21st April	Arrived at Portland from Newcastle (N.S.W.) (Over next few days some to-ing and fro-ing between Astoria and Portland).
	30th May	Sailed from Astoria for Queenstown (Eire) (Jenkins master).
	5th October	Passed east, the Old Head of Kinsale at 3.0 pm, bound for Queenstown.
	6th October	Arrived at Queenstown from Astoria with a cargo of flour.
	11-12th October	Sailed from Queenstown for Liverpool.
	14th October	Arrived in Liverpool from Astoria (Jenkins master).
	14th December	Sailed from Liverpool for Valparaiso (Thomas master).
1887	Speakings:	16th January 9S 32W steering south, all well.
	28th February	Arrived in Valparaiso from Liverpool (75 days).
	5th March	Sailed from Valparaiso for Iquique.
	15th March	Arrived Iquique from Valparaiso.
	4th April	Arrived in Pisagua from Iquique.
	9th June	Sailed from Pisagua for Aberdeen (Thomas master).
	17th August	Passed east Brow Head 1 p.m.
	Speakings:	8th September, 48N 28W Pisagua for Aberdeen, all well, by the *North Anglia*.
	23rd September	Passed east Dunnet Head, 1 pm.
	26th September	Arrived in Aberdeen from Pisagua.
	2nd November	Cleared from Newcastle (U.K.) for Valparaiso.
	4th November	Sailed from Shields for Valparaiso (Thomas master).
1888	24th January	Arrived in Valparaiso from the Tyne.
	26th January	Sailed from Valparaiso for Huasco (Thomas master).

	26th February	Arrived at Iquique from Huasco.
	24th April	Sailed from Iquique for United Kingdom or Continent (Thomas master).
	Speakings:	13th July 11N 27W – no ref.
	1st August	Passed east – Old Head of Kinsale (2.40 pm) from Iquique.
	2nd August	Arrived in Queenstown from Iquique with cargo of nitrate.
	6th August	Sailed from Queenstown for Hamburg (Thomas master).
	14th August	Arrived in Hamburg.
	21st October	Sailed from Hamburg for Valparaiso (Thomas master).
	22nd October	Sailed from Cuxhaven for Valparaiso.
	30th October	Dungene – passed west (10.0 am).
1889	22nd January	Arrived at Valparaiso from Hamburg.
	28th February	Sailed from Valparaiso for Caleta Buena (Thomas master).
	7th March	Arrived in Caleta Buena from Valparaiso.
	17th April	Caleta Buena – cleared for Hampton Roads.
	26th July	Arrived in New York from Caleta Buena; cable dated July 28th 1889: *"British Barque Dryad, from Caleta Buena arrived here 26th [July] reports:- on May 4th in lat. 32.30S, long. 89.12W, had very hard gale from S. W., with terrific sea; shipped a sea which washed away the two after boats, gutted the forecastle, started the forward house; bent the after skids and did considerable damage about the deck; again off Cape Horn had another gale, and carried away the steering gear."*
	2nd October	Cleared from New York for Melbourne (Thomas master).
	29th December	Arrived in Melbourne from New York.

Extracts from the MELBOURNE ARGUS, dated December 31, 1889.

THE DRYAD

The Dryad, an iron clipper which arrived on Sunday evening, is from New York with a full general cargo. The Dryad is of Liverpool build, and she is a vessel of over 1,000 tons. Until recently she rated as a ship, but in accordance with these days of economic sailing, her rig has been altered to that of a barque. The conversion does not appear to have crippled her sailing capabilities in any way, for the passage she has just concluded is one of the fastest which has been accomplished between New York and Melbourne for some time. The log book shows a very interesting record of good steady work done in running down the easting, where for 27 days the Dryad averaged 210 miles a day, the best day's work being 278 miles. The Dryad, it may be mentioned, crossed the line well to the westward, and afterwards it took her all her time to scrape along the South American coast without tacking. Captain Thomas, who has command of the Dryad, reports sailing from New York on October 5, and falling in with light variable winds, which continued until reaching lat. 31 deg. 7 min. N., and long. 39 deg. 17 min. W., where they were exchanged for the N.E. trades on October 21. Fresh breezes carried the barque comfortably along to lat 4 deg. N., where the winds became unsteady, and light variables were met with until November 3, when the trades set in. The equator was crossed on November 4 in long.34 deg.W., and in the first of the S.E. trades the winds were well southerly to lat. 8 deg. S., where a little more easting was infused into them. They continued from the S.E. quarter as far as lat.31 deg. S., and long. 20 deg. 20 min. W., where they shifted round to north-easterly on November 20, and were of moderate force from this direction until crossing the prime meridian on November 26 in lat. 38 deg. 48 min. S. The winds then came away westerly, and the meridian of the Cape of Good Hope was crossed on December 1, in lat. 41 deg. 45 min. S. in tracking the great Southern Ocean Captain Thomas made his easting on the parallel of 44½ deg. S., and along this line of latitude the Dryad had a sequence of fine, steady, whole sail breezes, which just suited her, and of which due advantage was taken. Cape Otway was passed on December 28, and the Heads were entered yesterday after a smart passage of 84 days. The Dryad arrived in port clean and in first-class order. Messes H.P. Gregory and Co. are agents for the vessel."

* * *

BARQUE DRYAD, from NEW YORK
This vessel having been berthed at Port Melbourne town pier and reported at the Customs, CONSIGNEES are requested to PASS ENTRIES, present bills of lading, and pay freight to the undersigned without delay. Value of dollar, 4s. 2d..
Consignees are hereby notified that unless they take delivery of their goods when landed, entries will be passed for them by the undersigned and stored at consignees' risk and expense.

H.P. GREGORY and CO., agents, 499 Bourke St.

CAPTAIN WM. THOMAS, of the above vessel, will not be responsible for any debts contracted by any of his crew while in this port without his written authority.

* * *

1890	3rd March	Sailed from Newcastle (N.S.W.) for Coquimbo (Thomas master).
	3rd May	Arrived at Iquique from Newcastle.
	Speakings:	5th September 'off Cape Horn' – steering east – by the *Glenesslin.*
	19th November	Arrived in Queenstown from Iquique with cargo of nitrate.
	25th November	Sailed from Queenstown for Leith (Scotland) (Thomas master)
	28th November	Passed east Lizard – no time stated.
	29th November	Passed up Channel past Prawle Point, bound for Leith from Iquique and Queenstown.
	1st December	Signalled off St Catherines Point (I.O.W.). Iquique for Leith.
	5th December	Signalled off South Foreland.

	13th December	Arrived at Leith. Report under 'Marine Intelligence'. *"The Barque Dryad of Liverpool from Iquique, while entering Leith Harbour on Saturday, collided with one of the Dock Commission's mud punts, knocking a large hole in her own Starboard bow."*
1891	3rd March	Sailed from Shields for Valparaiso, with a cargo of coal (Thomas master).
	9th March	Beachy Head – passed west 9.30 am. Moderate easterly gale, rain, cloudy.
	11th March	Dartmouth. *"News arrived last evening that there were some vessels ashore in Start Bay, but, the weather was so terrific it was impossible to go down, either by land or sea. This morning we went down in a tug and found that a steamer, name unknown [The Marana] was completely wrecked off the Start and all lives Lost, supposed to be a foreigner; also the iron barque Dryad of Liverpool, all hand lost. The schooner Lizzie Ellen of Chester, two lives lost and two saved; and the three masted Schooner Lunesdale of Barrow, the captain only saved. Of the last three, only a few spars and the fore-part of the hull of The Dryad are to be seen"*.
	12th March	Torcross. *Barque Dryad total wreck near Start Point, Start Bay. Captain's certificate picked up, also five bodies. Lost morning of 10th, not able to communicate before.*

Studying the above list, it will be seen that *Dryad* travelled the world from her home port of Liverpool to other parts of Europe, Australia, India, South and North America and sometimes rather out of the way places such as the Falkland Islands.

She was, after all, a cargo vessel with a total enclosed space of 106,900 cubic feet, giving her a gross tonnage of 1,069 (100 cubic feet to one gross ton). I can only find one example of her carrying passengers and that was on the journey from New York to Sydney in May to September 1879 – Messrs Lockrey and Brown.

I was surprised to see that the cargo was not always listed in the reports of arrivals and departures, but sometimes bulk cargoes were listed: wheat, flour, nitrate, barrels of cement, coal, that sort of thing. It must have been quite a task cleaning out the holds between voyages. Sometimes I was fortunate in obtaining reports from local newspapers and these appear above. They clearly illustrate the variety of materials carried.

Chapter Six

THE CREW AND THE AGREEMENTS

In an earlier Chapter I wrote of the day I traced the crew agreement for *Dryad's* last and fatal voyage. Before a ship set sail, the captain for the trip had to fill in one of these Board of Trade sanctioned forms. There was one for ships engaged in the home trade and one for foreign going ships. As one might expect it is a document in which details of the vessel, owner, captain and crew are entered, together with the geographical limitations to which the ship may sail. The crew, in turn, signed to say they would undertake to perform their chosen duty, be it captain, mate, carpenter, steward, able seaman or whatever. The crew also agreed to certain conditions, for example "to conduct themselves in an orderly, faithful, honest and sober manner". "No grog allowed" being another common condition. The apprentices, who had signed separate indentures, were "to be taught the business of a seaman". I shall return to this in more detail later.

Eleven of these agreements were to emerge, ten of them from the Memorial University, St Johns, Newfoundland, and these latter were concerned with earlier voyages; involving captains prior to Captain Thomas.

There were four captains all told:

1. JOHN EVANS (Cert No 89502)
   Born Tenby, Wales circa 1834
   Voyages 17/12/1874 Liverpool through to 19/6/1885 Hamburg.
2. ________ BRADBRIDGE (Cert No ?) Born ?
   One voyage only 6/4/1883 Cardiff? To 30/6/1883 Iquique.
3. ROBERT JENKINS (Cert No 21721)
   Born Scilly Isles in 1834
   Voyages 24/8/1885 Hamburg through to 14/10/1886 Liverpool
4. WILLIAM THOMAS (Cert No 900700)
   Born Trevine, Wales 23/2/1843
   Voyages 14/12/1886 Liverpool through to 10/3/1891. Drowned at Start Point, South Devon.

It will be seen that the longest serving captain by far was Captain John Evans with ten and a half years. I have tried to trace details from possible descendants, but to no avail. I even wrote to dear old Charlie Chester on his BBC Radio 2 "Sunday Soapbox" programme, but that did not produce any worthwhile results either. However, it was worth a try; after all it was a way of asking around five million people about 'my' ship at one go.

One of the pleasures of reading through documents such as the agreement and account of the crew, if you have a good sense of imagination like me, is that it can bring things to life, much as it did while I was wandering around the *Balclutha* in San Francisco. A simple piece of description such as the "distance in feet and inches between the centre of the disc showing the maximum load line [the Plimsoll line] in salt water and the upper edge of lines indicating the position of the ship's decks above the centre, . . . 3' 10''", conjures up thoughts of the ship rolling in heavy seas, with seamen on the deck leaping up to grab the lifelines to avoid the breaking sea. Captain Thomas writes in one of his letters home about *"having a swim along the deck"* in such conditions.

The agreement specifies the number of "sailors" engaged for each trip and states that they "hereby agree to serve on board the said ship [i.e. the *Dryad*] in the several capacities expressed against their respective names on a voyage from . . .". there then follows an outline of places that they might legitimately sail to, for example:

> *"Liverpool to Calcutta and any ports and places in the Indian, Pacific and Atlantic Oceans, China and Eastern Seas, thence to a port for orders in the continent of Europe, if required and back to a final port of discharge in the United Kingdom, term not to exceed three years. ——— - ".*

Other voyages would have similar descriptions, bearing in mind that navigation vagaries, varying weather conditions, mishaps, etc. could land a sailing ship a long way from its intended destination.

There is then a section which details the exact number of the crew, for example ". . . it is also agreed that the crew shall consist of mate, carpenter, bosun, steward, cook, seven seamen and seven apprentices . . ."

There is also the 'let out' for people 'not up to scratch' ". . . If any person enters himself as qualified for a duty, which he proves incompetent to perform, his wages shall be reduced in proportion to his incompetency."

The "scale of provisions" table is pretty standard and Table 1 shows what was agreed for the *Dryad's* final voyage.

On the following pages of the agreement there were 20 spaces for the crew to sign and for those unable to write this was done with a simple 'X'. Should the crew exceed 20 in number, then pages 3 and 4 would contain the signatures up to the maximum number of the crew.

Alongside the names there was a space for the age, town or county where they were born, the ship in which that person last served and the year. The cause of leaving the last ship was also entered, usually being "discharged" but quite often "deserted". In the comparatively rare event of an accident, then details of that were entered on following pages under the heading of "Certificates or indorsements (sic) made by consuls or by officers in British possessions abroad".

A typical example was that of able seaman James Kelly, aged 26, of Liverpool. He was taken on board as an extra hand on 19th February 1877; having arrived in Calcutta on 1st June

Food issue from Agreement and Account of Crew (PR Office, Kew)

"In addition to a daily issue of lime and lemon juice and sugar or other antiscorbutics" each crew member was allowed

"3 qts Water, 2 ozs Sugar, $^1/_2$ oz Coffee and $^1/_8$ oz Tea".

In addition the following were allowed for each man:

SUNDAY	MONDAY	TUESDAY	WEDNESDAY	THURSDAY	FRIDAY	SATURDAY
Bread 1 lb Beef $1^1/_2$ lbs	Bread 1 lb Pork $1^1/_4$ lbs Flour $^1/_2$ lb	Bread 1 lb Beef $1^1/_2$ lbs Peas $^1/_3$ pint	Bread 1 lb Pork $1^1/_4$ lbs Flour $^1/_2$ lb Peas $^1/_3$ pint	Bread 1 lb Beef $1^1/_2$ lbs Flour $^1/_2$ lb	Bread 1 lb Pork $1^1/_4$ lbs Peas $^1/_3$ pint	Bread 1 lb Beef $1^1/_2$ lbs Rice $^1/_2$ lb

"In any case an equal quantity of Fresh Meat or Fresh Vegetables, may at the option of the master, be served in lieu of the salted or tinned meats or preserved or compressed (sic) vegetables in above scale".

Substitutes: "At Master's option".

Table 1

1877 he decided to leave (with Captain John Evans' agreement), as opposed to jumping ship. The entry reads as follows:

> *"I certify that James Kelly has been discharged and left behind at this port on the alleged ground of mutual consent, and that I have enquired into the allegation and find it correct and that I have accordingly granted my sanction to his being so left. His balance of wages R56 – 6 – 0 paid to him and effects delivered.*
> *Signed D.J. Shipping Master. Calcutta, the lst June 1877.*
> *Stamped Govt. Shipping Office, Calcutta.*

An example of desertion which occurred in Sydney, Australia, 5th November 1879:

> *"Deserted – 3"*
> *"I hereby certify that the within named Maurice Fitzgerald, Michael Anderson and Geo. Wilson have been left behind at this port on the alleged ground of their having deserted, that I have inquired into the matter and find that the allegation is true, and that a proper entry of such desertion in the official log book has been produced to me"*
> *N.E. Shorter Shipping Master.*

In the case of illness, crew members were often left ashore although one wonders if they might have fared better aboard ship. Alone and probably with very little money and nowhere to go, they were at the mercy of individuals who took pity on them; or the seaman's mission if they were lucky. Two such cases of sickness occurred during the *Dryad's* voyage to Calcutta in 1876, John Pyle (Steward, age 21) and Gerrald Finerty (Seaman, age 32) both stayed ashore.

> The Shipping Master *"Certified that the under-mentioned seaman have been left behind at this port on the ground of their inability from illness to proceed to sea in the vessel. Their balance of wages paid in this office and effects of G. Finerty has been deposited in this office and J.W. Pyle has taken away his effects with him"*
> *J.W. Pyle R169 – 11 – 10*
> *G. Finerty R56 – 2 – 1*
> *Calcutta* *signed and stamped*
> *The 17 April 1876* *? — ? Shipping Master.*

In the case of illness of the captain, then the ship was stuck in port, since it is very unlikely that there was anyone on board, or indeed in port, who was sufficiently qualified to replace him. Such an incident occurred while the *Dryad* was bound from Cardiff to Iquique in 1884. I quote from Lloyds List. *"22nd August. Arrived at Stanley, Falkland Islands, with Captain Evans ill." "Stanley (F.I.) September 12th. The Ship Dryad . . . Is still detained here; Captain Evans being too ill to be removed at present". "19th September" "Sailed from the Falkland Islands for Iquique (Evans master)"*. No mention is made of the nature of his illness but it stopped the *Dryad* for nearly a month in Stanley. Apparently Captain Evans did another complete round trip from South America back to the UK and then on to Hamburg in June 1885. This is the last time Captain Evans was mentioned and the next trip, (Hamburg to Sydney, Australia), *Dryad* was under the captaincy of Robert Jenkins. As I wrote above, John Evans vanished without trace.

A seemingly unlucky voyage was that from London to Calcutta and on to New York undertaken from January 1878 to March 1879. Two crew were killed in separate incidents at different ports.

The first incident was when apprentice Richard H Hare fell into the ship's hold and fractured his scull (sic). The Calcutta Shipping Master records:

> *"... I see no grounds for any suspicion. His wages and Effects to be accounted for in the United Kingdom". 28 November 1878.*

Richard H Hare was part of the very first crew (as apprentice) on the *Dryad* on her maiden voyage Liverpool to Newport, December 1874.

Later, in New York, the second vice consul records:

> *"I also certify that it has been reported to me by the master that John Pinwell (Steward) while returning on board the vessel at this port, fell between the wharf and the ship and was drowned; That an entry to that effect in the Official Log-book has been produced to me; and that his wages and Effects are in charge of the Master, the vessel being about to proceed to the United Kingdom."*
>
> *G. Fraser*
>
> *2nd Vice Consul [no date]*

No comment is recorded as to the state of the steward as he returned to his ship, but I would wager a modest sum that alcohol had some part in his misfortune!

Sometimes a crew member may go missing at sea, perhaps fallen or washed overboard. There is also the likelihood that a man might loose his footing when aloft, or be catapulted from the rigging in heavy weather. Captains could not turn back in rough seas and sometimes accidents occurred unwitnessed. This may have happened in the case of Jusef Jansen, aged 40 years, from Finland. He disappeared on 15th October 1890 recorded in the agreement under the column *"cause of leaving ship"* as *"at sea, supposed drowning"*.

The potential crew for the *Dryad's* last voyage assembled in late February 1891 at South Shields. She had been loaded with coal (and possibly some small assorted items of cargo) for a voyage bound for Valparaiso in South America.

All the crew signed on 25th February 1891 except for the sailmaker William Irvine who signed a day later. They all had to be on board by 6.00 am on 27th February.

Two potential crew members, Harry Dhalberg and A Andersen failed to show up, so two substitute ABs (seamen) W. Lindsay and Karl Erikson were signed on on the day of departure from South Shields, that was 3rd March 1891. In total the crew numbered 21, under the control of Captain William Thomas.

It will be seen if the crew list is studied (See Table 2) that there are 13 British and 8 Scandinavians. Captain Thomas openly admitted he did not like using Southern Europeans because they *"cowered huddled together below decks in storms at sea"*. He much preferred the hardier Northern Europeans.

One of the items Captain Thomas had to check and sign for on the agreement was the distance between deck and plimsoll line (maximum load line) at 3' 10", not a lot considering the type of seas the *Dryad* could expect around Cape Horn.

Apparently the ship picked up a Tyne pilot who was to guide them down the North Sea

CREW LIST

DRYAD SOUTH SHIELDS TO VALPARAISO 3 March 1891

		Place of Birth	Age	Pay per month	Name of previous ship if known	Discharge Date
Master	William THOMAS	Pembroke	48	Unknown	ACONCAGUA	1886
Mate	J E Glanville	Dublin	30	Unknown	HELEN	1891
2nd Mate	W J Orford	Leicester	22	£4-10-00	GLASSENDALE	1890
Carpenter/Able Seaman	Carl Lange	Sweden	38	£5-10-00	CAMELO	1891
Steward	George Pattison	Dover	45	£5-00-00	BLUE BELL	1890
Cook	David Heilbron	Newcastle	24	£4-00-00	MERCIA	1890
Sails/Able Seaman	William Irvine	Paisley	55	£5-00-00	STAR OF PERSIA	1890
Able Seaman	G C Patterson	Denmark	28	£3-10-00		
Able Seaman	A Krone	Norway	20	£3-10-00		
Able Seaman	R Runsburg	Olasund	23	£3-10-00		
Able Seaman	A Pettersen	Copenhagen	21	£3-10-00		
Able Seaman	P Svane	Copenhagen	22	£3-10-00		
Able Seaman	A Larsen	Copenhagen	21	£3-10-00		
Able Seaman	J Flood	Dundee	25	£3-10-00		
Able Seaman	W Lindsay	Jersey	21	£3-10-00		
Able Seaman	K Erikson	Finland	38	£3-10-00		
Apprentice	Arthur Edward Borrill	Kingston Upon Hull	17	)		
Apprentice	Charles Henry McGarry	Cork	19	) Depends on length of		
Apprentice	Alfred Ford	Hull	16	) apprenticeship,		
Apprentice	Arthur Willian Fletcher	Dublin	16	) Total £30-00-00 over 5 years.		
Apprentice	Frank Marsdin Smith	Hull	16	)		

Table 2

and into the English Channel. There was a great deal of confusion with regard to the fate of this gentleman which I shall discuss a little later.

At the time of her wrecking, the *Dryad* carried 21 crew including five apprentices. (See Table 2). Two of these, Arthur Edward Borrill and Alfred Ford were only 14 years of age when they signed their indentures, although that was several years previously. The other three Charles Henry McGarry, Arthur William Fletcher and Frank Marsdin Smith were each 16 years of age at their signing.

Apprentices' indentures were on a standard form, a rather bleak document which stated the conditions of the apprenticeship succinctly. An extract of part of the document serves to illustrate the point:

> *"During the term of five years from the above date (date of signing), said Apprentice covenants that he will faithfully serve his Master and his Executors, Administrators and Assigns, and obey his and their lawful commands. Keep his and their secrets ——— will not embezzle or waste the Goods of his Master, his Executors, Administrators, or Assigns. Not to frequent Taverns and Alehouses, (unless on his Master's business), nor play unlawful games.*
>
> *In consideration whereof, the said Master shall use all proper means to teach the said Apprentice, or cause him to be taught the business of a seaman, and provide the said Apprentice with sufficient Meat, Drink, Lodging, Washing, Medicine and Medical and Surgical Assistance, and pay the said Apprentice as follows: First year £4, second year £4, third year £6, fourth year £6, fifth year £10. The said Apprentice providing for himself all sea-bedding, wearing apparel and necessaries. If apprenticeship expires at sea or foreign port, then said Apprentice to be rated on the ship's articles at the same rate of wages as the A.B.s were shipped at in England."*

Plate 15

This photograph of some of the Dryad's *crew was taken in Liverpool sometime between 1886 and 1890. It features Capt. Wm. Thomas (seated centre) and other crew members whose identity is not known, but the seaman on the right wearing a bowler hat would have been an officer. The man standing second left is likely to be the carpenter or sail maker as he is wearing a white apron appropriate to his trade. Judging by the age of the two young men at the front, they were probably apprentices. Many of the clothes worn by the sailors are ill fitting and probably second hand as seamen were poorly paid. In contrast, the Captain is wearing smart, well fitting clothes with a bowler hat, bow tie, long frock coat and highly polished shoes.*
Courtesy: Thomas Family, Pembrokeshire.

Plate 16

An essentially similar photograph to that in Plate 15 except that Capt. Thomas has stood down, and the owner of the Dryad, *Mr. John Bankes Walmsley (lower figure in the pale grey suit, extreme left, main deck), has entered the scene. Note centre figure, seated, with his right index finger pushed into his clay pipe. Note also bearded seaman with apron sitting on a fire bucket bearin the first four letters of the ship's name.*

Courtesy: Thomas family, Pembrokeshire.

Chapter Seven

CAPTAIN WILLIAM THOMAS AND FAMILY

William Thomas was born on 23rd February 1843 at Mesur-y-Dorth, Haverfordwest, Pembrokeshire. He was the son of Jane and Thomas Thomas, farmers, of Bryn Bank Croesgoch.

Little is known of his early life, but it is known that he joined a ship at Milford Haven in Pembrokeshire "at a very young age" and was away for two years. At first he was a cabin boy. He was lucky to have a very good master who left a marked impression on him. It is known that he attended marine college at both Cardiff and Bristol at some stage, but no further details are known. The first definite record of his merchant service was that he obtained a single mate's ticket (number 90077) at Bristol on 30th March 1869 at the age of 26. He

Plate 17 North End Trevine – Captain and Mrs Thomas's old house, apart rom the double glazing, essentially the same as it was a century ago.

progressed to first mate aboard the *Yosemite*, a 768 ton vessel owned by the Liverpool firm of J B Walmsley & Co on 4th July 1880. This was the company he stayed with for the rest of his life, progressing to captain aboard the *Aconcagua* (496 tons) on 8th May 1884. He was to remain master on her until taking over the captaincy of the *Dryad* on her voyage from Liverpool to Valparaiso, begun 14th December 1886. He was thus master aboard *Dryad* for four and one quarter years all told.

William Thomas married a local girl, Martha Lewis. They had been sweethearts since they were very young but she only saw him on his visits about every two years or so. They were married at Llanrhian Church in 1872. Their only child, Margaret, was born on 29th August 1874 (the same year as the launch of the *Dryad*) at the family home, Llannoy. They were able to purchase their own house (North End, Trevine) in 1878 following the deaths of Martha's parents, with some money they had inherited. (See Plate 17).

It is interesting to note that Martha's two brothers both went to sea as young men and both 'jumped ship' in Australia and fled to the goldfields. Later both returned to Wales and became successful and well known farmers in Pembrokeshire.

Captain Thomas was a sober and God fearing man who had the reputation of being a good navigator and a strict but fair man to his crew. He also liked things 'just so' and enjoyed fine attire. He always liked to have a real silk handkerchief and when he had new collars he

Plate 18
Captain William Thomas taken in Melbourne early January 1890 and referred to in his letters home 2nd and 31st January 1890.
Courtesy: Thomas family, Pembrokeshire

Plate 19
Captain William Thomas and Mrs Martha Thomas and their daughter Margaret, taken around 1884–6 on a tin-type or Ferrotype, a type of photograph much used in Victorian times by itinerant street photographers (note the rusting around the edge). It was the only photo that Maggie had of the three of them and she treasured it very much.
Courtesy: Thomas family, Pembrokeshire.

would pick at them and tease out a thread or two from the edge so that people would see they were real fine linen not just cheap cardboard imitations. A glance at Plate 15 shows how smart he was. As mentioned earlier in the book, no visitors were allowed to roam the deck without first having their shoes inspected for deck-damaging nails.

Captain Thomas was apparently rarely at home, even when the *Dryad* returned to a UK port. His wife and daughter would often travel to be with him when the *Dryad* was in dock or anchored off awaiting unloading/loading of cargo. She would sometimes sail to Hamburg for orders and it is reputed that Margaret actually attended school there on occasions. Once when *Dryad* was in dry dock Margaret went down into the dock and removed some of the large barnacles which had grown on the hull when in tropical waters. These were later mounted and are still in the possession of Mrs Mary Jenkins. (Plate 20).

Margaret was something of a 'tomboy'; one ship's master asked Captain Thomas if he knew his 'lad' was up the rigging and was quite surprised when informed that the 'lad' was in fact a lass. Nevertheless, Margaret was capable of being frightened, since on one occasion (aged 16) she and her mother had just returned from visiting *Dryad* in Germany and Margaret had been left in charge of their trunk at Whitechapel Dock. She sat on it while her mother went off in search of a cab. While she was away, Margaret's eyes fell on a paperboy's headline billboard, "Jack the Ripper strikes again". Margaret was acutely aware she was in the "Ripper's" operating area and was terrified, every second seeming like an hour until Mrs Thomas returned.

Mention was made earlier of Captain Thomas's letters kept by his family in Pembrokeshire. Although only ten survive, they make interesting reading. Over the years the

Plate 20
Barnacles from the Dryad's *bottom!*

paper has become fragile and the writing somewhat faded. A couple of pieces of the much folded and unfolded paper have been lost, but the majority are complete and readable. Many of the letters are factual but the loneliness and frustration of being away from home for long periods comes through.

I have tried to keep to the original spelling and punctuation. Mrs Mary Jenkins (Captain Thomas's great granddaughter) said that his spelling and grammar were poor. Maybe so by today's standards, but he was probably considered well educated in his time. Quite a number of his fellow crew members on the *Dryad* were unable even to sign their own name and this is shown by the number of times they signed on the crew agreement with a cross.

It is interesting to note that the captain was always formal, addressing his letters "Dear Wife" and signing off "your affectionate Husband". Only rarely did he write of personal matters. On one occasion when Martha Thomas had been out to New York to see her husband (August/ September 1889) she left a very personal letter in the chronometer case. This delicate instrument was in the sole charge (and probably ownership) of the captain. Mrs Thomas knew that only her husband would look in there. His reaction to finding it can be seen below. Regrettably a small piece of the letter has been torn out. Mary suggested that what was written was so personal that Margaret ripped out those couple of lines to prevent anyone else reading them and so maintain the secrecy of their words of love. What a loyal and loving daughter she must have been. I was very pleased when a member of the '*Dryad* Diving Team' found the chronometer key, lying where you might expect, in the 'Captain's Cabin

Plate 21
Margaret Thomas as a schoolgirl, aged about 12.
Courtesy: Thomas family, Pembrokeshire.

Gulley'. It is a strange and wonderful feeling to hold it in my hand and know that Captain Thomas used this self same key time and time again to wind his clock, and to know that this artifact can be linked to one of his letters home.

Life at sea in the nineteenth century was not only difficult but hazardous. Out of the 262 ships Roydens built, 129 ended up wrecked or missing, so if this figure is representative of shipping generally at that time, a seaman had roughly a one in two chance of shipwreck. Captain Thomas must have been very aware of the dangers of his profession and he often refers in his letters to being spared to get back home. In some ways the letters are quite stereotyped. His "nothing strange to inform you at present" was almost a catchphrase.

When Captain Thomas sailed from South Shields on 3rd March 1891 he had intended it to be his last complete voyage. He had expressed the intention of emigrating to Australia with his family upon returning to Liverpool. There was even a rumour about the purchase of a plot of land. It is said that Captain Thomas was baptised in the chapel of his home village at Croesgoch, where his parents were buried, possibly sometime in 1889, something he had always wanted.

Mary and her brother Ron have done a great deal of searching but it seems as though the other letters have not survived. I am very grateful for those that have. They are reproduced below, with their kind permission.

Plate 22

Two envelopes containing letters home from Captain Thomas; one from Melbourne, Australia, the other from Chile. It is interesting to note that although they are both addressed to the same destination, in the letter from Chile he writes the address Pembrokeshire [via] England, but in the one from Australia the address is [via] Europe.

Barque "Dryad"

15 days ahead of "Yosemite" Valparaiso, 3rd March 1887

My Dear Wife

I am glad to inform you that I arrived safe here on the 28 Feb after a fine passage of 76 days I had a hard gale on the Sunday after I left L.pool but I did not feel it much as I had got out clear of the land. and acording to promise I let you know how the Dryad is behaving after the very bad character she got. but she is not so black as they painted her but the first Sunday after I left she took a sea on board and knock mee down and I had a swim along the deck. but I think that the "Yosemite" being before mee had something to do with that in causing me to give her the whip rather to hard. but I would not care if I had a swim every Sunday all the way out, so long as I gained my point which you see I did do, as I told you I would, and I suppose you seen what happens to my other antagonist the "Samanco" that vessel of Mr. Wakeham that sailed from Birkenhead the day before I sailed how she got on shore about tuskar. I must be passing there about the time. going along beutifull on the whole I must say that the "Dryad" is a Noble Ship and will go past Everything, and I am very pleased with her. I am sorry to inform you that the Coleara is bad hear at "Valparaiso" but I hope that I shall soon be away from hear as I had a telegram from Mr. Walmsley this afternoon to sell the coal for what I could get for them so I think that they will be sold tomorrow to be discharged at "Iquique" or "Pisagua" so I shall soon leave this place, so I shall have to lay 4 days at Quintero Bay in quarantine before I can proceed to blow the sicness off "Quintero" is a little place about 18 miles out side of this so you see it is very bad here at preasant. but I hope that the Lord will spare us all to leave this place safe when there is so many Dying. but not from the ships it is all in the town so I have nothing strange to inform you at preasant hoping this will find you boath quiet well as it leaves mee at preasant. there is ships arriving here now that left home before I or about the time that I left home to go to L.pool and the "Yosemite" has not arrived yet nor the "Aconcagua" so I must conclude with my kindest love to you both.

I remain your affectionate husband and father

Wm Thomas

I hope you have seen my arrival for I wiered home and got an answer this afternoon. I have got no Letters yet nor I dont think that I will get any now for I shall saile before the maile come in so I dont expect to get any so if I dont dont you expect many

P.S write to mee to "Iquique" I expect that I shall go there of Pisagua and I can get the letters sent down

adress

J. Englis & Co.

"Iquique"

Barque "Dryad"
"Iquique" 20th March 87

Dear Wife

I take the oportunity once more of addressing you these few lines in hopes that they will reach and find you in good health as I am, happy to say they leave mee at preasant. I am glad to inform you that I recived your letter yesterday, and happy to find that you are quiet well. I sailed from "Valparaiso" on Saturday 5th. March and arived at Quintero Bay on Sunday or next day and had to remain there four days to blow the Colera of before we could go on to "Iquique". So I sailed from there on the 10th. and arrived here on the 15th. after a fine passage and I am going to discharge 500 Tons here and the remainder I got to take to "Pisagua" where I hope to load Nitrate for Europe but the ship is not yet chartered, but I expect to be soon. I dont know whether the "Aconcagua" and the "Yosemite" has arrived yet they had not on the 11th. of this month. About my new ship I like her very much she is a fine vessel. I should like to meet with that old Peggy now to see if she could pass me the same as she did before. I dont know what to say about your nighbours behaviour in quarelling and fighting I supose that they are no longer together.

I have not recived no papers nor the books only the letters if you had send them a few days sooner so that I could get them before I left "Valparaiso" I might get them. I have nothing strange to inform you at preasant hoping this will find you both well. That Wm. Davie is here Captn. Bowen that sailed from Antwerp the same day you remember. I hope you have seen my arrival before this as I Telegraphed home from "Valparaiso" there is no mail by Panama for the Peruvian ports is closed against any ships or steamer from Chile. So I have nothing strange to inform you at preasant hoping this will find you quite well, and I hope that you will keep clearof those quarels and disturbances of the village for they are a Disgrace to a Cristian Country, and I think it is time to keep the Missionaries at home when Father and Son is fighting. So please have nothing to say in their Disbutes and you will greatly oblige your affectionate Husband

Wm Thomas

Barque "Dryad"
"Pisagua" 4th. May 1887

My Dear Wife

With pleasure I take the oportunity of writing you those few lines in hopes they will reach and find you both well as they leaves me at preasant. I am glad to inform you that I am nearly done discharging my outward cargo and will soon commence loading Nitrate for home. I am now waiting for some Nitrate for ballast before I can finish discharging the coal. I Shall be very glad when the coal is all out it has been a long job we have to put all the coals in bags and saw them up and then weigh them so can gues how much work wee have got to fill 1600 tons. of coal in bags and saw them all and weigh them, all before wee can get clear of them but I am glad to say that they are all nearly out. I hope to be sailing from here early in June hoping to have a good Passage home. I have not got an answer from you yet to the letter I sent on my arrival at "Valparaiso" it ought to come soon now. and you ought to here by Telegram that I sent to Mr. Walmsley & Co on the lst of March and had an Answer back on the 3rd. and you ought to here by that and if you did I ought to have a letter long before this. I received by last Steamer your letter writen on the 24th. Feb you might have writen one day sooner so that you would write it on My Birth day. and give mee a birth day preasant I wrote to Magie by last Steamer So I hope to here from you soon again I remain Dearest Wife your affectionate

Husband

Wm Thomas

Barque "Dryad"
"Pisagua" 2nd. June 1887

Dear Wife & Daughter

With pleasure I write you those few lines to inform you that I am once more nearly ready to sail for home. but I am sorry to inform you that I am going along way from you this time. for I have got my orders to direct to "Aberdeen", in Scotland and you will not hear or see nothing of mee pasing no place untill I arive at Aberdeen for I intend to go round the North of Ireland and through the "Pentland Firth" and I am not very well pleased to be sent up that way but must go hoping this will reach you all well as I am hapy to say it leaves mee at preasant, I expect to be loaded on Saturday 5th. June and will saile on Monday or Tuesday. but I shall write again before I saile. I have nothing strange to inform at preasant

I remain your affectionate

Husband & Father

Wm Thomas

Barque "Dryad"
"Iquique" 21st Ap 1888

My Dear Wife & Daughter

I am glad to be able to inform you the "Dryad" is loaded once more and will Saile on Tuesday if all is well for Falmouth or Queenstown for Orders where I hope to see you both come this time I have had a very good dispatch in loading and I hope I will get a good Passage home. I see that the "Stanley Sleath" is at "Pisagua" loading the "Addaleed Mary" in here since last Sunday and is close to the Dryad and I see also that the "Niad" has arrived at Colquimbo & "Yosemite" at Valparaiso

So I have nothing Strange to inform you at Preasant hoping this will find you both quite well. I did not get a letter from you by last mail but I will be here for one more and I hope to get one then but I will not have time to write after this letter. you had better write to me to Falmouth and Queenstown for I will go where ever the wind is Fair c/o Fox & Co Falmouth & S. Scott & Co Queenstown I have posted a letter with copy of crews account to you by this mail also. pleas keep them, I hope I wont be sent to such an Outlandish place this time

I see in your letter that Mr. James is in hopes of getting a ship I hope he will get her. as you say the Captn was astray at "Iquique" it is very Easy to get astray here and I dont suppose that he is the first one. and you should not be to hard on those poor Captains for their lifes is not a very pleasant one

I remain your affectionate
Husband & Father

Wm Thomas

I send you a list of all the ships at "Iquique" there is very few here now and it is a good job or I would not be loaded yet
it is now spanish.

Barque "Dryad"
New York 16th. August 1889

My Dear Wife,

With great pleasure I write you these few lines in hopes that they will reach and find you in Good health and full enjoyment as they leave mee at preasant. I have not received no letter from you since my arrival hear and is waiting to hear from you day by. You had better start for "New York" as soon as you can for there is no hope of the "Dryad" coming home this time. I expect will go to "Melbourne" or "Valparaiso" again, so please write if you are coming out for we wont be long. Mr T.I. Walmsley came here by last steamer. Hoping to here from you soon.

I remain your affectionate Husband

W Thomas

Barque "Dryad"

My Dear Wife

I feel very sorry to leave you this time, but trusting that we shall be spared to reach one another again safe on my arrival home. I seen your note in the Chronometer box and it has made feel more than ever for you. I now ask you pray for me that I may be kept to return safe home once more as I should like to see Maggie once more. I write this in tears. When I find this old room empty I kept up all night until I came

(a piece of the letter is torn out here)

if you come down before dark look out for the "Dryad" as wee will not be very far I send back (?) alie $58 for you. Get them changed before you sail. Good By My Dear Wife and God Bless you and may you have a safe and a pleasant passage home.

Barque "Dryad"
Port Melbourn 2nd. January 1890

My Dear Wife

With pleasure I write you those few lines in hopes that they will reach and find you in good health as I am at present I arrived here safe on 29 Decr after a very fine passage and a good quick one as you will see by the report of the Melbourn paper after leaving New York again I very nearly blew all my flags to pieces trying to attract your attention when you was passing close to in that big steamer I suppose the poor little dryad was beneath your notice. I seen you or rather I could see the Passengers walking back and fore the Deck you was so close I cant understand you not see my flags when you was passing. I recived your letters on my arrival here. I thought there was a mistake somewhere an I found where I had made some mistake but keep the papers untill I return home so that I can compare them again. I suppose you have hered of the Dryad s arrival as I sent a Telegram to L.pool on my arrival here. I have seen J. Phillips I sent him a letter and he came down on new years day to see me he looks well and is getting stout and looks very helthy and is in good spirits, and I have promised to go up and spend the Sunday with them next Sunday their not living far from the ship I have sent Magie a letter to H. West by this same mail

I seen that Barque Hiram that was laying the other side of the dock after I was out 15 days and I arrived here on the same day as that ship that left for Melbourn before the "Dryad" commence loading – so you see the "Dryad" has been showing them what she can do this time. I don't know yet where I am going to from here but I hope that I shall get to England this time I remain Dear wife your affectionate Husband

W Thomas

I hope to here from you soon again.

I send Magie a pice of paper the same as this but I don't know if the advertisement is at the bottom of it, as I think I told her I could not find a place to take my likeness and I just seen this advertisement at the bottom so if she will notice it I am sold nicely.

Barque "Dryad"
Port Melbourn 2nd. Jan 1890

My Dear Magie

With pleasure I write you those few lines in hopes they will reach and find you well and happy. I recived your letter on my arrival hear. I arrived hear on Sunday last 29 day Decr just in time to have the New Year here this is a grand place I wish you were here to se it. I got J. Phillips Adress in your letter so I droped him a note so he came down and saw mee on New Years day. and I have promised to go and spend next Sunday with them. I don't think you now him now he is so stout and look well and healthy and in good spirits. I have not seen any more people here that I know but there is a lot of people here from the old Country and a Welsh Church which I intend to see next Sunday. it is very warm weather here and fine being the Middle of the Summer here, and the Ladies sporting their white dresses untill farther orders, in Parties and Excursions across the Bay and by rail, the Colonial people are great people for keeping up the Hollydays, you ask mee for my likeness I cant promise you as you now that I don't care about going to the trouble to look for a place to have them taken. now about the passage I had a fine passage out this time and some go as you will see by the Enclosed report cut from the Melbourne Argus of 30th Decr 1889 so you can see that the "Dryad" has done some good work this time and arrived the same day as the American Ship that left New York when I commenced to load, I don't now yet where I will have to go from here but I hope that I shall fetch home in England somewhere next time so I must now conclude wishing you a hapy New Year and that you are enjoying yourself and remember when you are dancing and rompsing about, to be Carefull and not forget that your poor Father is under you. on the underneath part of this old globe and nearly right under your feet. but living in hopes to clime up again someday on a level with you, so:

Good By My Dearest
Maggie and God Bless You and mind and be a good girl

You see that the "Dryad" has been going down at the rate of 210 miles per day. and will if spared come up again at the same rate some day.

I don't know if you are still at school. I hope you will get on with your learning as soon as you can and your Music I remain your affectionate Father

W Thomas

Barque "Dryad"
Port Melbourne
31st. January 1890

My dear Wife,

With great pleasure I take this opurtunity of writing you these few lines in hope that they will find you in good health as I am at present. I expect to be discharged and sail from here about the middle of next week for Newcastle and then load a cargo of coal for West Coast of Valparaiso for orders, I expect so you had better write to Valparaiso as soon as you receive this letter and send some papers and adresses c/o Duncan Fox & Co. Duncan Fox & Co. dont forget, I intend writting Maggie by next mail before I leave here. I have nothing strange to inform you at preasant hoping your feeling well as I am at present time. J. Phillipe and wife and little boy is quiet well and wishes to be remembered to all at home. I shall be there on Sunday evening and I had promised to go last night but did not go. I am getting tired of that place now I am getting a dispatch here. I received your papers by last mail after long waiting

Photograph yesterday getting the shape of my good looking face taken for Maggie so you will see what sort of a job they will make of it, and let me know when you write to Valparaiso what Maggie thinks of it I remain my Dear Wife your affectionate Husband,

W Thomas

P.S. When you receive this write to Valparaiso and write every fortnight until you receive my letter from there. Trusting to God to bring us safe there and home some day.

W Thomas

Chapter Eight

START POINT AND HALLSANDS

Start Point

Start Point is a sharp headland forming the extreme south-east tip of land which skirts Start Bay in Devon. It is one of the most exposed peninsulars in England and together with the dangerously shallow Skerries Bank to the north-east causes the wise skipper to give the area a wide berth. To the casual observer on one of the high grounds in the area, Start Point headland might appear to run north/south, but the further south it goes the more it curves eastwards, so the tip runs virtually west/east. (See Fig 5 and Plate 23).

The origin of the name has been the subject of some debate. To the 'landlubber' the name is a corruption of the Anglo Saxon word steort meaning a tail. There is another Steart Point in the south-west of England, in north Somerset. This is also a narrow curving spit of land, but much more low lying than its South Devon namesake. However, to the deep sea merchantman Start Point was literally that – the start of their real voyage across the oceans to remote parts of the world.

The sharply ridged finger of rock sticking out into the English Channel has beckoned many a ship into its wrecking clutches in the past, and it is surprising that a lighthouse was not erected there before 1836. There is no record of a traditional brazier or beacon burning there to warn ships of the potential danger, and the lighthouse that stands there today is the original one designed by James Walker. At the time it was considered a fine building with its gothic style architecture and battlement-like parapet around the light. The lighthouse itself is a rugged building of square hewn rock some 92' (28m) high (Plate 24). In 1977 it was listed as a building of special architectural or historic interest under the 1971 Town and Country Planning Act. The light stands 203.4' (62m) above mean high water level (which coincidentally is exactly the same measurement as the length of the *Dryad*) and as such, is one of the highest lights in Britain. Naturally the facilities have been constantly updated over the years, but the basic 1836 building is still there, although parts of the ancillary buildings were severely damaged by storms in December 1989 battering the cliff base. The foghorn and associated pump room were effectively destroyed as they hung at a precarious angle on the cliff edge (Plate 25).

Obviously the *raison d'etre* for the lighthouse and fog horn was to warn ships of the presence of Start Point itself, but in 1836 the light alone was too weak to penetrate any but the thinnest mist. Consequently a warning bell was fitted in 1862. Following an incident in 1901 when a

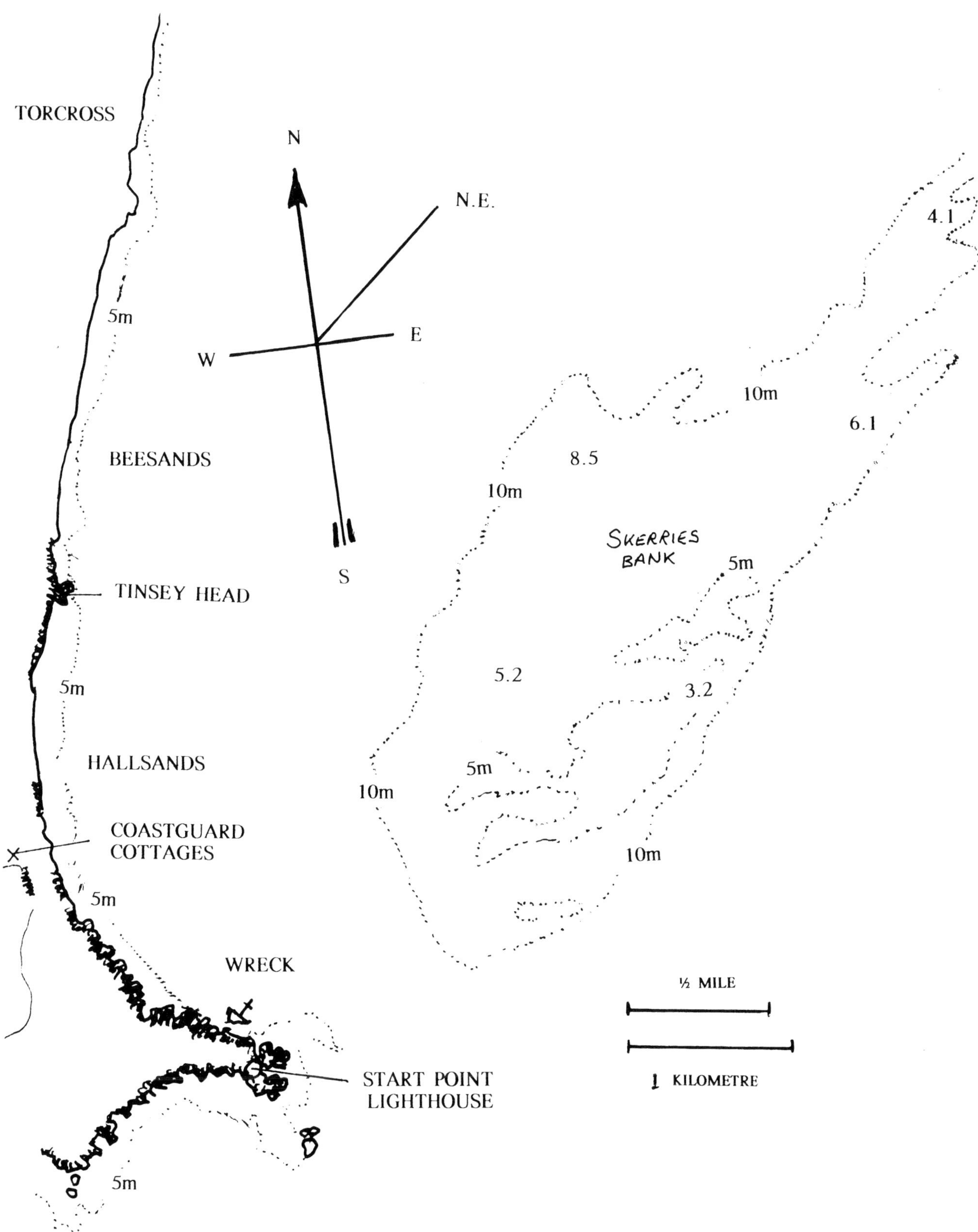

Fig. 5
Sketch showing the position of the Skerries Bank relative to Start Point and the approximate position of the wreck site, together with associated land marks and mean low tide levels.

Plate 23
Start Point viewed from the north.

ship stranded on the low rocks at the foot of Start Point, a new, incandescent lamp was fitted. As a result of technological developments, a yet more powerful petroleum vapour lamp was fitted in 1922 and six years later still a radio beam was added to the warning devices. Following the installation of electricity in 1959 the light was again updated to a 1500 watt filament lamp, which can be seen under good visibility some 25 miles. None of these things would have helped the poor *Dryad* however, as so far man has been unable to harness storms.

The fog signal bell was replaced in the late 1870s by a siren, and this in turn by a very powerful fog horn in 1928. In recent years this has been driven by powerful diesel-engined compressors, but prior to the late sixties when these were installed, there was a system whereby a heavy weight falling captive in a tube down the cliff face operated a mechanism, bringing about the audible signal.

Plate 24
Start Point and lighthouse viewed from the air.

Plate 25. (Photo Brian Tanner)

Plate 26
Start Point on the western side. The paired black rocks to the right are the Blackstone, against which the Marana *collided a few hours before the* Dryad *was lost around the eastern side. The remains of the* Marana *lie a short distance away towards Lannacombe.*

On several foggy days when I have been unable to dive, I have walked down to the lighthouse when the fog horn has gone off; sounding rather like a wheezy giant drawing breath, followed by a shattering bellow which literally made the ground shake. (There is even a warning about it on the gate). Alas, it was most of this apparatus which suffered as a result of the 1989 storms.

Following an automation policy by Trinity House in the 1980/90s, the keepers in light ships and houses round Britain were replaced by electrical and mechanical means. So it was with Start Point Light. She went automatic in 1993, and the process nationwide was completed with the North Foreland Light in Kent in November 1998.

It was one of the Start keepers, keeping watch on the night of 9th March 1891, who saw the *Dryad* loom out of the storm just moments before she smashed headlong into the precipitous cliffs, just as a few hours earlier Mrs Briggs had watched the *Marana* come round the corner and go to pieces on the Blackstone. (See Plate 26).

Hallsands

Start Point viewed from Hallsands is a spectacular piece of scenery. I first went to Hallsands in 1960 whilst on a field trip at university. I was struck by the prettiness of the place and found the history of the old fishing village fascinating. I read the publications on the locality, taking in the nearby villages of Beesands and Torcross, and revisited the area on several occasions. I began to get to know the region quite well.

Plate 27
South Hallsands taken in the late 1890's before the dredging which removed six hundred and fifty thousand tons of shingle from the shallow shore causing the loss of the protective beach and consequent destruction of the village by storm in 1917. Note coastguard cottages on cliff top.

Some years later, as a lecturer, I took my own groups of students down to the South Hams, staying at the Slapton Ley Field Centre and the youth hostels at Bigbury on Sea and Salcombe. Various aspects of field biology reinforced my knowledge and love of the South Hams. I liked the place so much I used to come here on holiday, staying in bed and breakfast accommodation, hotels and even camping; eventually moving here.

Sometimes in the evening we used to travel out to the Hallsands Hotel for a pint or two. It had rather a strange atmosphere and was run by three elderly ladies, one of whom used to dress as a city gent, short hair cut, pin-stripe suit and all. I believe they had a theatrical background and the bar was decorated with numerous photographs of various celebrities. Apparently they were known as "les girls". We never stayed there then.

As the 'Grim Reaper' took his toll of the girls, new owners took over, namely David and Carole Light, who became good friends over the years. David was a diver and ran the hotel as a base for divers as well as ordinary visitors. The fact the hotel had a compressor for re-charging air cylinders and a couple of inflatable dinghies for hire made it an absolutely ideal

Plate 28
Hallsands beach.

centre. The beach at Hallsands was a good place to launch and load boats from since it was composed largely of pea sized gravel – sort of inbuilt ball bearings to run a boat ashore with heavy diving kit aboard. It was usually a safe anchorage as well.

The position of the hotel, perched as it was on the side of the cliff, provided an ideal lookout from the dining room, especially from a window seat. It became our base for years.

David had a wide knowledge of dives and diving in the area, gleaned not only from his own experience, but from long chats over the bar at night, exchanging tales and information with the multitude of divers who have undergone the Hallsands Hotel experience. I always used to impress on David the importance (from my point of view) of not mentioning to others anything about the *Dryad*. As far as I could tell, he never let me down, so I used to slip into the compressor shed and show him my bag of finds for the day. We had the occasional dive together and he was with me one March day when I found the Jack Staff socket (Gallery 4) in the clearest visibility I think I ever experienced at the Point.

I have many happy memories of the man, his unmistakable laugh and his habit of calling all us blokes "my boy". When one asked for a half pint of beer in the bar it was nearly always a full pint – what he referred to as a "Hallsands Half". The Dire Straits record of 'Sultans of Swing' will forever remind me of happy evenings in the bar – it was the first number on the record which Dave used to play as background music when he entered for his evening session of being barman. Next came the pouring of a drink for himself, followed by the ceremonial unwrapping of his first small cigar for the night.

Sadly he was taken ill with cancer one late autumn and died just before Christmas; a great shock and a sad loss to his wife Carole and their son Tristan and all who knew him. Diving in the area would never be the same again. Almost fittingly, the hotel began to fall prey to cliff top erosion and ceased to exist as such. An era over if ever there was one.

Plate 29
Hallsands Hotel with compressor shed in foreground.

Plate 30
The Hallsands coastguards, together with their families, pose outside their cottages around the turn of the nineteenth century. These buildings, necessarily occupying their cliff-top position for observation purposes, escaped the destruction wreaked upon the beach level village by the storms of 1903–4 and 1917. They are virtually unchanged today, although now occupied privately. The coastguard on the right in the picture takes his post seriously, with smart dress and a telescope under his left arm. In contrast, the man second left is more relaxed, with his pipe and two ferrets! Photo: Fairweather collection.

Chapter Nine

THE STORM AND THE WRECKING

Blizzard details

Although the latter part of 1890 had been characterised by hard frosts both in Britain and the continent, the early part of 1891 had been relatively mild. Indeed, many in the west country could not remember such a warm and spring like February with rainfall for Devon and Dorset recorded at less than 0.1inch. March opened with rather changeable weather with rain and wind, but on the ninth of March a deep depression came up the English Channel from the South West, so much so that the centre of the depression was some 90 millibars below the high pressure areas on the continent. Thus to fill this depression cold air, precipitating snow, rushed in from the North East. This hit unsuspecting ships and their sailors all along the south coast of England, causing them to either run before the storm or seek such shelter as they could find. Within 24 hours, over sixty ships had been wrecked; at least four of which met their doom along the two mile stretch between Beesands and Start Point.

The north easterly hurricane would have driven any ship in Start Bay straight into the cliffs, or possibly the beaches at Beesands and Hallsands. North east also happens to be the approximate longitudinal axis of the Skerries. It is debatable whether any ship 'lucky' enough to be driven ashore on a beach in the area would have fared better, although rescue of shipwrecked mariners may have been made slightly easier due to better access. No such crumbs of comfort existed for the crew of the *Dryad*. Although there is a lighthouse on Start Point, the driven snow would have reduced visibility to mere yards and doomed vessels probably hit the cliffs or submerged rocks before anyone knew how close they were to disaster.

The storm was such that all postal communication was stopped for a week, telegraph wires and poles were blown down, roads blocked and trains stuck in deep drifts, and the whole district was cut off from the outside world. In order to gather information and report on the conditions, a local newspaper editor and correspondent, Mr Jas. Fairweather, decided to see for himself the conditions around the South Hams, his reports formed the basis for a remarkable book which he published, entitled "The Blizzard in the South Hams of Devonshire: being a record of the great storm of Monday and Tuesday, March 9th and 10th, 1891." The following extracts from Mr Fairweather's account vividly illustrate the severity of the storm.

"Monday, 9th March opened with a strong north-east wind, which increased in violence as the day advanced. About mid-day rain and sleet commenced to fall, and early in the afternoon it was snowing heavily. The wind between four and five had risen to a strong gale, with frequent hurricane squalls, which drove the snow flakes in all directions, and made it very difficult to get about or see objects at any distance. The storm was perfectly blinding. It continued through the whole of the night, the snow falling very thickly, and the wind, especially at times, blowing terrifically."

"A large number of boats were moored off the quays and other places at Salcombe, but the force of the gale was so great that the sea became fearfully agitated, so that most of the boats were swamped and sank at their moorings, whilst some fared worse and were considerably damaged, in some cases past repair."

"The two Plymouth steamers – the KINGSBRIDGE PACKET *and* EXPRESS *– arrived in Salcombe about four o'clock in the afternoon, and it was with extreme difficulty they could be got alongside and away from the quays. Both these steamers made their trips to Plymouth, and it was fortunate that the wind was fair, for as it was they had a fearfully rough passage, scarce being able to see anything for the blinding snowstorm, and it was no easy matter to find their way into Plymouth, the crews of both vessels being agreed, that taken altogether, the voyage was the worst they had ever made".*

"The night of Monday was a terrific one; the wind blowing a fierce gale, the snow falling heavily, and trees and telegraph wires being blown down in all directions. It was not safe for anyone to be on the roads."

The damage done by the storm inland was described as *"devastation all round, greenhouses were broken in, roofs of houses demolished, trees uprooted and broken down, and shrubs destroyed".*

The farmers of the district all suffered losses, principally of sheep and lambs, and were engaged over the next two weeks in digging them out of the snow. In one case a local lad discovered a sheep alive after being buried for twenty days. Other losses included horses and fruit trees, all of which cost the local farming community a great deal of money.

On Wednesday, 11th March, the storm had abated, leaving the whole of the South Hams district under a thick blanket of snow. The average depth was reported to be around two feet deep, with drifts much deeper in parts. (See Plate 31). The wind having died down, the sea was calmer, although there was still a heavy swell.

In spite of the difficulties caused by the impassable nature of the roads, *"Mr Fairweather ———- determined to make an effort to get to Prawle, so as to gain full information of the casualties, and thus place the friends and others interested, and also the public, in possession of the facts at the earliest possible moment. He had been told it would be useless to attempt to get to Prawle, as every road was completely blocked, but he determined to make the effort, even if he failed, and on the journey was accompanied by Mr J C Nye, Deputy Receiver of Wreck, and Mr W T Snell, correspondent for the Western Daily Mercury at Salcombe".*

After a long and arduous journey the three men came to the Union Hotel (now known as the Pigs Nose Inn) where three survivors of the wreck of the steamship *Marana* were recovering from their ordeal. The *Marana* had been wrecked on Start Point just a few hours

Plate 31
Fore Street, Kingsbridge, around 11th March 1891.

before the *Dryad*, with the loss of 25 lives. Mr Fairweather was thus able to obtain full details of the wrecking at first hand. He later went on to Start and Hallsands to gather more information on the other wrecks of Monday night, making a total of four known wrecks and the loss of 52 lives, the greatest number known to have been lost on that stretch of coast in one event. All witnesses to the conditions at sea agreed it was the worst they had ever seen.

The wrecking of the *Dryad* happened in the very early hours of Tuesday, 10th March. She perished unwitnessed, save for those on board, but none of the crew lived to tell the tale. Local coastguards and lighthouse keepers were unsure as to exactly where the *Dryad* struck. From contemporary reports she hit the precipitous cliffs between the Start itself and a point some 500 yards to the north-west. What is certain is that she went to pieces very quickly, and only one piece of hull and a couple of spars were still visible the following day.

The steamship *Marana* was the first of the four vessels to be wrecked in the storm in Start Bay. She was seen by Mrs Briggs (the wife of one of the Start lighthouse keepers) to strike the Blackstone Rocks at about 5.35pm on the afternoon of Monday 9th March. The coastguards at Hallsands, Prawle and Torcross were all alerted and hastened to Start Point with life-saving apparatus, to see what assistance they could render the *Marana's* crew. Some three hours later the coastguards saw a light in the bay near Beesands and some went to investigate. The remaining men went back to Hallsands. The light apparently was from the schooner *Lunesdale* which subsequently stranded and broke up with the loss of four lives.

At approximately the same time as Beesands fishermen and some coastguards were trying to save the *Lunesdale's* crew, another schooner, the *Lizzie Ellen* went ashore near Hallsands. Again, some local fishermen attempted to effect a rescue, and did manage to save two crew members, but the captain and a boy were lost.

What with all the to-ing and fro-ing and the confusion and stress of that evening, the potential rescuers must have been very tired; not only coping with the wrecks, but the severe weather making movement between the sites difficult. Mr Jones, the head keeper of the Start lighthouse, was, however, still keeping watch after midnight, when he saw a ship's lights right close in by the headland. He ran to call the other keepers and together they made their way towards the place where Mr Jones had seen the lights. Mr Fairweather reconstructs the scene:

"*They (the keepers) proceeded down the cliffs at the risk of their lives, and it was only by holding on to each other that they were prevented from being blown away. When they got down they could not discover a vestige of anything, neither did they hear a cry of any sort. The coastguards of Hallsands say, at the same time as the lights were noticed by the lighthouse keeper, they say what they considered to be a steamer's lights just in the same position. The coastguards fired off a rocket and burnt a blue light to warn the vessel of her danger, but the vessel's lights were not seen for more than three minutes, when they disappeared. At this time the Torcross coastguards were at Beesands, and seeing the signal, they also proceeded to the Start, the Hallsands coastguards having got there before them. As the coastguards were coming back from the Start along the coast, they met the lightkeepers, who informed them of what they had seen. All the coastguards then strained their eyes to look and see if anything could be discovered. But they neither saw or heard anything but the roar of the tempest. Mr Crickett (chief officer of coastguards at Hallsands) said the coastguards did their utmost to keep their eyes open, and strained them in the face of the storm but the effort was so painful they had to desist. The force of the storm was so great their eyes seemed as if they were being pricked with needles, and they were bloodshot the next morning as the result of the strain they had been put to. No sign of the Dryad or any other vessel could be discovered.*

When the vessel's lights were seen, Mr Hewett [actually Mr William Hewitt, coastguard officer in charge of the life saving apparatus at Prawle], together with the apparatus, had left Hallsands for Prawle, and had got as far as Chivelstone Cross, when he was overtaken by a mounted messenger, who had been despatched by the chief officer of coastguards at Torcross, and desired to return at once to the Start to the assistance of a vessel gone on shore there. He returned to the scene of the casualty at half past two o'clock, and by that time the vessel had broken up, all her masts and spars were gone overboard, and but little of the wreckage could be discerned in the darkness."

In the morning only a small part of the hull and a couple of spars were to be seen and these were still showing the following day when a Lloyds reporter went to the scene of the wreck in a tug.

In my active diving days I would often pop in to see an old friend of mine in Salcombe, Malcolm Darch, the model shipwright. We used to indulge in much useful discussion about the *Dryad* and related maritime affairs. One such occasion was in January 1987. We were talking of the Fairweather book on the Blizzard of 1891 and Malcolm remarked that he knew Len Fairweather, Jas Fairweather's grandson. I said I would very much like to meet him.

Plate 32
Photograph of the remains of the Dyad taken on 11th March 1891.
Courtesy: Fairweather Collection.

Plate 33
Photograph of same scene as plate 2 but taken 11th March 1991 and including the author.

Following a telephone call a meeting was arranged for that very afternoon. Mr Fairweather greeted us most cordially. He said he had a copy of his grandfather's book and produced same in a few moments.

I glanced through the account, (some of which appears above and below) and was very pleased by what I read. In the back of the book there were a number of plain pages onto which had been pasted some photographs. Apparently this was a common practice in the nineteenth century as conversion and printing of photos was difficult. One photograph made a huge impact on me and I stared at it in disbelief. It was of a very familiar scene, that is the *Dryad's* wreck site, complete with wreckage. The photograph was not credited, but possibly was taken by Jas Fairweather himself.

I sought, and obtained, permission from Mr Len Fairweather to reproduce both extracts from the text and the photograph itself. I gratefully acknowledge that permission here. Sadly Len Fairweather passed away a few years ago. I would have liked to have given him a copy of this book by way of thanks.

The photograph does not show much detail, but two of the items visible in the picture are still in virtually the same position, over one hundred years later. (See Plate 32). In the photograph can be seen several pieces of wreckage. The dark angular piece (being 'pointed at' by the sharp piece of rock) is almost certainly part of the deck house, with several spars and pieces of sail on the surface. Assorted flotsam and other debris may be seen entrapped in the little cove showing bottom right.

I visited the scene exactly one hundred years after the wrecking (on 11th March 1991) to pay homage to the ship and her crew and although it was not a nice day, generally overcast with periods of heavy rain, the *Dryad* once more worked her magic. The sky cleared and the sun shone for a few minutes to enable a photo of the author to be taken. (Plate 33). Later at home, comparing the two photographs I noted the tide level was almost identical; quite a co-incidence with the tidal range there being around 20 feet!

There was some debate at the time as to the identity of the ship that struck close to Start Point that night. After a fruitless search for any signs of the wreck or survivors, a coastguard was sent from Hallsands at first light to make a detailed examination of the coast to see if there were any signs of the wreck. He found more than he bargained for, since he came across a shipwrecked sailor clinging to a rock. Mr Fairweather again:

> *"On a low and insulated rock, known by the name of John Hatherley's Nose, a man was discovered, who was lying on the rock, on his right side. On making this discovery the coastguard ran to the lighthouse for assistance, and the man evidently saw him, for he turned over on his other side, and watched the coastguard round, the latter pointing to the lighthouse, as a sign that he was going there for help. The lighthouse men were most prompt in their efforts, and responded willingly to every call made on them. Mr Briggs, one of the keepers, and Mr Pollybank the coastguard, then returned to the rock with ropes. They threw a rope on to the rock, which fell only a few feet away from the sailor. He saw it and then slid down, evidently with the intention of securing the rope, but he seemed afraid, and instead of slipping on to the lower ledge of the rock where the rope was, he climbed onto the top of the rock again, and laid himself flat on it on his face and hands. Those trying to rescue him, seeing how exhausted he was, got a ladder to get to him, but in throwing it out, the ladder struck the rock and broke in two. The sailor then seemed to lose his hold, and slid down, holding on to the rocks for several seconds, when he fell head over heels, and a heavy sea came and washed away the poor fellow who had weathered the night, and*

nothing more was seen of him; it is thought the night's exposure had so benumbed his limbs, as to have deprived him of all strength. Great doubts are expressed as to what vessel the sailor came from, for it seems almost impossible he could have got to the rock from the Dryad; and there was some wreckage visible near the wreck that did not appear to have belonged to the Dryad. The coastguards at Hallsands say distinctly that the lights they saw were a steamer's lights, whilst there is no doubt that the lights the lighthouse keepers saw were those of the Dryad. Only a piece of the bow of the Dryad were discovered in the morning, but a mass of broken wreckage was seen floating along the coast, and tons of it were washed out to sea by the next tide".

I think I can say with some certainty that the unfortunate sailor was a member of the *Dryad's* crew. It is most unlikely that he could have been from the *Marana*, since they were swept westwards from the Blackstone Rock, and in any case were round the other side of Start Point (the lee side) compared to the *Dryad*. (See Plate 26). Although it may be true that the rock on which the man was found was some distance from where the *Dryad* struck, a large piece of the after part of the starboard side of the *Dryad* lies against the bottom of the rock called 'John Hatherley's Nose'. (See Plate 34) The floating wreckage could have come from the two wooden ships ashore at and near Beesands.

I believe the Hallsands Coastguards were mistaken in believing the lights they saw were from a steamer; and that the Start lighthouse keeper was correct in identifying the ship as the

Plate 34
The rock known as John Hatherley's Nose.

Dryad. As Mr Crickett said, the snowstorm was so bad as to make it difficult for coastguards to keep their eyes open, so they may be forgiven for misidentifying lights over a distance of more than a mile in those conditions.

It has been suggested that if the *Dryad* did strike the Skerries bank, she would have done so violently, causing some of the masts and spars to crash down, taking with them some navigational lights, and maybe altering the ships light pattern into one reminiscent of a steamer; thus causing the misrecognition on the part of the Hallsands coastguards.

Speculation arose as to which wreck various bodies were from, and that is all it can be, save for the three men washed up on Hallsands beach and who were later positively identified. Some days after the loss of the several vessels, inquests were held. I have tried my best to locate the reports but none has been forthcoming. Of these, some information about the *Marana* was published by Mr J Fairweather in his account of the blizzard, but nothing about the *Dryad.* So I have to turn to the Kingsbridge Gazette for information about the bodies recovered. There was an inquest at Hallsands (probably in The London Inn) held on Sunday, 15th March 1891.

Altogether eight bodies were picked up – washed ashore at Hallsands – five of the bodies were placed in the London Inn stables and three in the coastguard station at Hallsands. Some of the bodies were much disfigured, which made identification difficult. One such was believed to be Charles Henry McGarry, an apprentice, whose uncle travelled to Hallsands but was unable to give a positive identification, having to telegraph to the lad's home for further details. Two other apprentices were identified, Alfred Ford by his father and Arthur Edward Borill from tattoos on his body. A much older man, William Irvine 55, who was sailmaker on board, was identified by his brother in law, but had a highly distinguishing feature in that he had a cork foot. These last two mentioned sailors are part of the eight buried at Stokenham Churchyard whose graves are marked by a stone, readily seen today. (See Plates 36 & 37). Until fairly recently there was a memorial stone for Alfred Ford, close by that for William Irvine, but this has now been removed.

I was naturally keen to obtain a copy of the full inquest on the *Dryad.* In my searches through various sources it seemed strange that the *Marana* inquest was reported in detail in several publications but only in outline for the *Dryad* event. Perhaps this was because there were survivors in the case of the *Marana,* but none for the *Dryad.* When I was assembling this book, Kingsbridge's Cookworthy Museum increased its database with the acquisition of much local newsprint on microfilm and new equipment with which to read it. I had hoped this would reveal the inquest details I was looking for. One local paper promised "2 very full reports of the wrecks at Start Point .... and full reports of the inquest." "At last", I thought. When I arrived at the date of the issue I was seeking there was a blank screen, followed in huge black capitals by "ISSUE MISSING". Greatly disappointed, there was nothing I could do about it. So I carried on twiddling knobs and found this in The Gazette, Friday, March 20, 1891.

> *"Inquest at Hallsands"*
> *"Mr Sydney Hacker, county coroner, held an inquest at the London Inn, Hallsands, on Sunday last [15th March] on the bodies which had been found. The Jury comprised Messrs Thomas Bucknill, (foreman), W. Bastard, George Ridge, Robert Prettyjohn, Samuel Loggin, John Steer, J. Hawkins, Rennells, W. Stone, W. Quick, W. Kelland and G. Pulleyblank.*
>
> *Irwin(sic) was identified by his brother in law. He was the man with a cork foot, and was a sail maker on board the Dryad. Alfred Ford, who was only 17 years of age, was an*

apprentice on board the same ship, and was a native of Hull. He was identified by his father. Evidence was given by Mr Frederick Crickett, Chief Boatman, in charge of the Hallsands station as to the wrecking of the vessels as detailed above, and further evidence was given as to the finding of the bodies.

The coroner in addressing the jury alluded to the fact that there was no life boat or rocket apparatus between Prawle and Brixham, a distance of twenty-five miles, and he suggested that the jury should recommend that something of the sort be provided and kept near Hallsands.

The jury returned a verdict in accordance with the evidence and endorced the suggestion of the Coroner that a life-saving apparatus should be kept near Hallsands.
The two bodies which were identified at the inquest were interred in Stokenham churchyard on Sunday, five were buried on Monday, and one on Tuesday."

Plate 35
Board of Trade Rocket Life Saving Apparatus at Island Street, Salcombe, in the early twentieth century. Possibly this was set up (as others were) in response to the Coroners remarks at the Dryad *inquest with regard to the need for such an apparatus in the vicinity.*

Not a great improvement on the snippets of information previously given. A yellowed piece of paper in some boxes of 'shipwreck' odds and ends bears the note . . . "Devon record office states some 19th century records missing (due to enemy action in WWII?)".

It is interesting to note that the Gazette for Friday, 3rd July, 1891 records another body washed up on the beach at Lannacombe Mill (less than a mile away from Start Point) and was buried at Stokenham, like the others.

There is no doubt that the wind and sea that fateful night were savage, and once the *Dryad* had gone to pieces, the fragments were scattered over some distance. The direction of the wind at the time (east north-east) would have blown any moveable wreckage along the coast and effectively into the bay. A number of contemporary reports said the shore was strewn with wreckage from Beesands to Prawle Point but it is certain that this came from a number of wrecks as well as the *Dryad*. Being of iron construction most of the body of the ship would have sunk. Some parts were wood of course, such as the decking, ship's boats, and possibly the uppermost yards. The deckhouse, too, was largely wooden. Two of these items can be seen in Plate 32, but it is very doubtful whether these travelled far, weighed down as they were with iron fittings, not to mention the fact they were connected to the rest of the rigging by steel and rope shrouds.

Some of the decking is still on the seabed, fastened to the remains of the hull, but after a hundred years there is very little left. (Gallery 19). In trying to 'reconstruct' the ship as she now lies, I have often puzzled as to where parts of her have gone. I have yet to find the anchor or the heavy studded chain. There is only one lower mast down there when there should be three, let alone the topmasts, t'gallants and royals. These last two would be most vulnerable in a heavy grounding, but for the rest?

Mr Alan Viner (latterly Head of the Department of Ships at the National Maritime Museum in Greenwich) told me that after the second world war, several sweeps of the sea bed in the area were made to clear wreckage that could have been hazardous to shipping. It is possible some of the missing parts were lost in this way, but as a sweep involves a wire being pulled by two vessels it is doubtful if they would come so close to the cliffs as to trawl *Dryad* remains. It is also possible that some pieces of iron may have been salvaged to help the war effort sometime between 1914 and 1918, or 1939 to 1945, but I have not the slightest scrap of evidence to support this hypothesis.

At the time there was considerable speculation as to the cause of the loss of the *Dryad*. One contemporary rumour, that there was a Tyne pilot on board and that he told Captain Thomas that his compass was out by several degrees, have not been substantiated by any of my research. Several other rumours such as the position of the *Dryad* when she struck, varying from 100 yards to 500 miles (sic) from Start Point, the fact she was burning steamers' lights, that 24 crew were aboard; that she was carrying several different cargoes, have all fuelled the speculation and helped to confuse the issue. What is virtually certain is that no one will ever know the true story.

If I am permitted my 'two pennyworth', I would like to dismiss the 'pilot still on board' theory. Why would a Tyne pilot still be on board an ocean going vessel at the very mouth of the Atlantic Ocean hundreds of miles away from his home port? This did happen on occasions when foul weather overtakes a vessel and the pilot has no option but to go with her, but the weather up to the 8th March was nothing out of the ordinary. Quite often pilots heading westward would be dropped off at Beachy Head, but this is not mentioned in Lloyds List, simply a standard sighting "9th March – Beachy Head – passed west 9.30 a.m." Secondly, Captain Thomas was such a meticulous person I doubt very much if he would have undertaken any voyage knowing his compass was out by two points. I am convinced he would have headed for the nearest port to have the defect checked, and, if necessary, rectified. It could be argued that events overtook the good captain and his ship but the wrecking occurred a full six days after *Dryad* left port to commence her journey and although the weather was changeable with some wind and rain, it would not have prevented the ship heaving to and getting the compass checked before the hurricane struck. Surely it would not have taken a competent pilot six days to spot a faulty compass?

I believe the most likely explanation was the simple one, that is that the *Dryad* was blown off course and fell foul of the Skerries. This is a very shallow shingle bank. (See Fig. 5) She bottomed and had her rudder unshipped, or torn off. (The *Dryad's* rudder was designed to be unshipped when the vessel was afloat and this would have made it easier for the rudder to become detached accidentally). Thus unable to steer, she was blown before the storm into the cliffs of Start Point. A glance at Fig. 5 shows the feasibility of this argument. A portion of the stern of the ship lies against the base of the cliffs, but there is no sign of the rudder. Furthermore there is a large piece (80' long) of her keel and bottom plates some distance away from the wreck site showing signs of an after part having been torn off, suggesting perhaps she had bottomed and split up. A survey of the Skerries by an experienced team of divers might answer this question, but it would be a difficult and hazardous undertaking which I am NOT recommending here.

Two additional extracts from south western newspapers at the time are reproduced below:

EXTRACTED FROM 'SOUTH WALES DAILY NEWS' FRIDAY MARCH 13TH 1891.

LOSS OF A BARQUE AND ALL HANDS

"During the gale on the South Coast, the iron barque Dryad, of Liverpool, was lost with all hands. Intelligence of the sad disaster only reached the owners in Liverpool on Thursday morning, the telegram conveying the melancholy fact being received from Exeter, to which place it had been conveyed by train from Dartmouth, telegraphic communication with the latter place having broken down. The Dryad left Shields on the 3rd inst. for Valparaiso with a cargo of coals. She was reported as having passed Beachy Head on Monday last. Late on Monday night, when the hurricane was at its height the Dryad foundered, being driven ashore at The Start. Coastguards from a distance observed the barque in deadly peril, but were powerless to assist, and all on board the ill-fated vessel perished. There was not a chance of rendering succour, the cliffs at this point being so high and precipitious that unless a vessel runs into one of the very few coves there is absolutely no opportunity for rescue. The Dryad, which was a fine iron barque, carried a crew of 24 hands. She was owned in Liverpool, and was built in 1874. Her commander (Captain W. Thomas) was a native of Trevine, Pembrokeshire. The crew who signed articles at the South Shields Shipping Office were as follows:- Chief officer, J. Glanville, of Fowey; second officer, W. Orford, of Bosworth; carpenter, Carl Lange, South Shields; steward, George Pattison, South Shields; seaman David Heilborn, South Shields; Wm. Irvin, ditto; George Patterson, ditto; A. Cronie, ditto; A Petterson, North Shields; P. Svane, South Shields; A. Harsen, ditto; G. Flood, Dundee; W. Lindsay, of Jersey; K. Erick, and A. Fine, apprentices; A. Borrell, C. McGarry, A. Fletcher, J. Smith and A. Ford, belonging to

Hull and Liverpool. It is reported that a Tyne pilot was on board, but this is not accurately known."

EXTRACTED FROM 'EXETER FLYING POST' FRIDAY 13TH MARCH 1891

DISASTROUS SHIPPING
DISASTERS IN START BAY
WRECK OF THE *Dryad*
LOSS OF THREE VESSELS AND
TWENTY-EIGHT LIVES.

A Plymouth telegram says
"The coastguard, with the life-saving apparatus which had been to the Start in connection with the wreck of the Mirana, arrived in reply to a message, but were too late, the vessel becoming a total wreck. On their way back to Prawle they received information for a further wreck at Hall Sands, and returned at once, reaching the spot at half-past two on Tuesday morning. They found, however, that the ship had broken up, the waves having thrown up part of the forecastle, painted chocolate colour, with the name Dryad, in black letters. The vessel had left Shields Harbour on the 3rd inst. for Valparaiso, and was commanded by Captain William Thomas, of Treville, Pembrokeshire. Her crew, who signed articles at South Shields Shipping Office, were as follows:- Chief-Officer J. Glanville, of Fowey; second officer, W. Orford, of Bosworth; carpenter Carl Lange, South Shields; steward, George Pattison, South Shields; seaman, David Heilborn, Wm. Irvin, George Petterson, A. Crecie of South Shields; A. Petterson (North Shields), P. Svane and A. Harsen (South Shields,) G. Flood (Dundee), Lindsay (of Jersey),K. Errick and A. Fine (apprentices), A. Borrell, C. McGarry, A. Fletcher, F. Smith and A. Ford (belonging to Hull and Liverpool). It is reported that a Tyne pilot was on board, but this is not accurately known. It is feared that all are drowned. On Tuesday morning a man was seen lying on a rock called John Hatherleys, the rock being about five hundred miles (sic) north of the Start, and everything that could be thought of, ladders and ropes, were used to rescue him, but without avail, in consequence of the wind and seas. Subsequently the poor fellow, who is supposed to be one of the crew of the Dryad, was seen to be washed off and drowned. Two indentures were picked up on the beach. The coastguard at Hallsands reports that on Monday night he saw a large boat, supposed to be a mackerel boat, in the bay, but shortly after he lost sight of her. Among the wreckage on Tuesday morning the keel of this class boat was discovered, but no particulars are known. Five bodies have been picked up at Hallsands, and one of these appears to have had a cork foot."

Many of the South Western newspapers which gave reports of the wrecking say that a total of eight bodies were found in the vicinity, and from 15th March through to 17th March the vicar of Stockenham, Conrad Finzel, was a busy man, officiating at the funerals of ten people all told, although two people were locals and died of causes other than shipwreck. As the county archivist put it "burials of unidentified bodies washed ashore were quite common at the time in the Register." Two of the *Dryad's* crew who were positively identified (Irvine and Ford) were buried by coroner's order, on 15th March, their abode being entered as "wrecked on the Barque *Dryad,* Start Point, March 10th". Some doubt existed as to the identity of Borrill who was consquently buried a little later. The five unidentified were simply described as being "washed ashore at Hallsands" and interred on 16th March, also by authority of the coroner.

Plates 36 and 37
The graves of William Irvine (sailmaker) – left; and Arthur Borrill (apprentice) – right; in Stokenham churchyard.

Chapter Ten

THE ARTIFACTS

At the beginning of each year's diving activities, we had to swim over the wreck site to clear it of masses of seaweed and any other large pieces of debris, such as hunks of towrope, tangled trawl, broken fish boxes, etc. We also had to cut free long straps of kelp, which seemed to grow at an amazing rate each year. There is nothing more annoying when you are trying to concentrate on a tiny artifact than having your vision obscured by a large 'windscreen wiper' of kelp washing backwards and forwards over your mask, or something trying to tug your demand valve from your mouth. Once clear, investigations could continue.

To be honest, when I first swam about over the remains of the *Dryad* she was just another of the many wrecks I have been on, and a rather boring one at that. She was very broken up, and mostly hidden from view under the sea bed. The first few bits and pieces we came across were not any more interesting than the average 'souvenir' that any diver picks up during his/her travels over the bottom, bits of bottle, broken cups, that sort of thing.

Before long, however, items began to arouse interest, and just as a jig-saw puzzle becomes more interesting when you can link a few pieces together, so the accumulation of artifacts began to tell a story, especially when they could be related to human activities. We could imagine, for instance, the master of the ship using the parts of the sextant we recovered to navigate his charges across the oceans. One might visualise a member of the crew polishing a porthole, or looking through it at some exotic new place as the *Dryad* finished another journey. The victualling weights we found we could imagine being used to measure out the rations, or the cook preparing food. 'Swinging the lead' took on its original meaning once more as I chiselled out sounding leads from their concreted graves and imagined some member of the crew right up in the bows, casting the lead into the sea, and shouting the marks back to the helmsman. Rather pathetic personal items, such as cutlery, made me sad to think that once men ate their meagre and unappetising rations with these implements.

However my interest grew and, as I related in an earlier chapter, my prime aim was to identify the ship. The word got around that there was a wreck near Start Point and a lot of dive boats used to come over and anchor on the site. Luckily the wreck was not obvious and many people gave up after a little while pronouncing "there is nothing there". One chap I knew said he was going to "give Henry's wreck a good bashing" and get some goodies; what sort of things he thought he would find I do not know, but I was delighted when he surfaced after some 20 minutes declaring it was a waste of time and that there was "just a load of tot down there"! Panic subsiding, I was very pleased at this interpretation, and was happy to agree.

One potential problem was that the nature of the wreck site made it an ideal habitat for crabs and lobsters, and was therefore a favourite site for the local fishermen to lower their pots. I always made a point of approaching any crabbers or lobster fishermen in the vicinity and telling them my name and what I was doing. This was a bit of a risk in a sense because I never knew if they would tell other divers, but I felt it was a risk worth taking. Eventually they got to know me and realised that I was not out to rob them. Once or twice individuals were not so nice. I remember on one occasion a non-Mensa member asked me why I could not go and dive on my wreck somewhere else? On another occasion I was threatened with a filleting knife. The following day Martin and Robert came down with their inflatable and our two boats with four people aboard stopped the said gentleman with a pincher movement. Firmly, but politely, I explained what I was doing, told him I did not like his rather silly attitude, and after that we even got the occasional wave from him.

After a couple of years, things began to settle down and although occasionally we had 'visitors' asking if we were on the wreck, I was always non committal, although suffering duck's syndrome (all calm on the surface but paddling away like the devil underneath). We used to use a number of diversionary tactics, and they usually worked. We used to express great surprise: "What wreck?"; and enthusiastically: "A wreck! Really! Any gold coins?", and my favourite: "Can we dive with you?" That always used to send them muttering on their way.

I have dived on her solo on a large number of occasions (but always with boat cover). Sometimes people would enquire why I always went to the same place on my own. "Oh, I am a geologist taking samples", or "as I dive on my own I need to keep in by the rocks", or "I just enjoy paddling round in the shallows watching fish and taking photographs". There was an element of truth in all of these of course, and a few people did 'twig' what I was up to. As far as I can tell they did the decent thing and left 'my' wreck alone.

One summer's afternoon I had just surfaced from a dive and another solo diver approached me in his boat and we had a chat. From what he said I recognised this chap as a diver who had his own little project round the point and told him so. He acknowledged this correct identification with a smile, telling me not to worry about the *Dryad*, he was just interested in looking around the site. He would respect my work. He bade me farewell and I returned to base. The following morning I returned to continue my work and there on the edge of my excavation was perched a small heap of carefully arranged stones with a couple of pieces which my friend had found and put there for me. Thank you Terry.

It is unrealistic to hope that no one will dive the *Dryad* and remove material from her. As I have pointed out earlier, my long term aim is to mount an exhibition of her remains in order to bring to life a typical late nineteenth century ocean-going iron sailing ship. When I first registered my finds with the Receiver of Wreck as Salvor in Possession, I made enquiries with the Board of Trade as to how I could prevent people diving on her and removing objects. "That is a difficult one", said the man at the other end of the telephone. "You should buoy the site, together with an advertisement telling people to keep clear for, say, 100 metres radius as archaeological work is being undertaken. Also to advertise in local newspapers to tell people what is going on and please keep clear; and keep a watch on the site. Lastly to ensure you continue to work your claim on a regular basis, and keep the local Receiver of Wreck informed of your progress".

Some of this was not possible, and in addition was likely to be counter productive and draw attention to the site – something that I wished to avoid at all costs. I had to hope that silence, the difficulty of locating anything tangible to work on and the fact a great deal of hard, and frequently totally unproductive digging was required, would keep my project safe.

Once we started to find artifacts on the sea bed, I used to record their position on a piece of paper, then transfer that onto a larger master sheet. I have no formal training in archaeology, but as a zoologist my scientific training and the resultant "go carefully, record everything, do not jump to conclusions" approach has helped. By recording we had an accurate idea of where we had excavated, helped a great deal by the lay-out of the plates and frames of the ship. Sometimes more than half a year would elapse between one dive and the next; for example over the winter period when it was not possible to dive. Doing things systematically was a far better way of excavating and, as I was to discover several years later, more productive as many interesting pieces came to light only fractions of an inch above the bottom.

Perhaps it might be a good idea to define my 'base line' for delving downwards. Some of the excavations went down over 3', but mostly were 1' to 18". Where the overburden had accumulated over a hundred years or so, the fine gravel and sand had mixed with fragments of marine life, and as these had become buried and decayed they had left a grey stain to the materials. This meant that a change in colour of the bottom indicated that it was in position before the *Dryad* landed there. I never found anything below the 'demarcation' line. The fine overburden was loose and relatively easily wafted away by powerful strokes of the hand, much as you would do playing table tennis with an open hand, but no bat. One small problem with this technique was that the material soon built up and ran back in the hole. By noting carefully where we had been and filling the previous excavation as we went, it was possible to examine a reasonable amount of the sea bed. It also had the not inconsiderable advantage of filling our holes after us, so within a few days the bottom appeared undisturbed and did not advertise the fact that the *Dryad* diving team had been busy.

For the most part, the particles of the overburden were of micaceous rocks, comparatively light weight compared with artifacts. I would waft down to either bed rock or the 'demarcation' line (as above) where any object heavier than the minerals would settle. Many people will have experienced this for themselves, standing in shallow water on a sandy beach as the waves wash over their toes. In no time at all, you are sinking in. You might imagine how deep you would go after a century.

This knowledge prevented us from missing the carpenter's gold ring. One late season dive Martin and I were busy wafting deeply about ten feet from the edge of an iron plate in a rocky area which had been worn smooth and deep by many centuries of tidal flow. I was almost on the point of signalling to Martin that we should move elsewhere when I remembered the fact that small heavy objects work their way down deep. I knew we would not recover anything large as there was no room for it. Martin and I had our heads in a hole and with both wafting, the water was murky. There may just be a small interesting piece in the last remaining fractions of an inch of mud I thought. Now it happens that there are a number of universally used signals in the world-wide fraternity of diving, but we had a few of our own. A hand thrust out, fingers spread over the surface of the area being worked meant STOP, whatever you are doing, keep still, I think I have seen something! Martin signalled thus; I froze. We waited for a little while and a tiny semicircle of yellow appeared, maybe a curtain ring, or another cup-hook perhaps. Martin reached in and picked up a lovely gold signet ring. It was late in the day and getting quite dark so we could not make out any details. Back on board we saw the ring was engraved with the initials "C.L" – Carl Lange, the *Dryad's* carpenter. This find caused me more problems than all the rest of the artifacts put together, as I shall relate below. Honesty may always be the best policy in the end, but it can also be a blooming nuisance.

Carl Lange was a 38 year old Swede who had signed on for this voyage having recently been discharged from the *Camelo* of Glasgow. The ring was in perfect condition, without a scratch, cradled and protected by the soft silt into which it had rolled. I was surprised how small it was; it would not even fit over the middle of my little finger. I was very careful not to lose it. On examining the ring later, I discovered it had been assayed in Birmingham in 1890, the year before the wrecking. Maybe Carl bought the ring for himself; maybe it had been purchased by a wife or girlfriend as a Christmas present just weeks before he signed on for the fatal voyage. We will probably never know.

Plate 38
Carl Lange's ring.

When I sent my list of finds for that year to the Customs and Excise as declaration of wreck droit, the words "18 ct. gold signet ring" must have set the alarm bells ringing. Gold from a wrecked ship! It is not generally known that the laws governing salvage were made many years ago and that even the latest legislation is part of the Merchant Shipping Act of 1894. This Act requires that the Receiver of Wreck (who is usually a customs officer) has a duty to try to trace the owner of the goods salvaged. If this is not possible, then the Crown may claim the goods, and the salvor be rewarded for his efforts. In the old days (before enactment of the above law), the contents and fabric of a wrecked ship were often claimed legally or otherwise by the Lord of the Manor in which the ship came to grief. The actual owner of the goods had little or no chance of recovering his property. Sometimes gangs of people even used to set out deliberately to wreck ships by lighting false beacons and the like, so they might plunder the results of their cruel deeds. At the risk of ending up in the Tower of London myself, it seems as though not a great deal has changed, since if I wanted to keep Carl Lange's ring I had to buy it. In recent years it has often been the practice of the authorities to waive the Crown's claim to salvaged items if these are of little or no commercial value, and the salvor allowed to keep the findings in lieu of a salvage reward, provided that the salvor has behaved in a proper and responsible manner.

In order to be on the right side of the law, I have always declared everything I raised from the *Dryad*. The Customs and Excise people were always polite and helpful but, as you might expect, followed the letter of the law. They had to pass on the details of my finds to the Board of Trade. The gold ring stuck out like a sore thumb amongst the vast majority of the artifacts, and they wanted a valuation. So in all innocence I walked into my local jeweller's shop and had the ring valued for insurance purposes. I duly sent off the document to the powers-that-be and awaited the next move. I was staggered by the reply that they wanted £131.07 from me if I was going to keep the ring. I had made the stupid error of declaring the ring's replacement value and not the intrinsic value of the piece. I appealed and submitted a more realistic valuation based upon the gold content. Some weeks later having paid the dues (allowing for my portion of reward, plus of course Customs' commission and VAT) I had the ring, safe, sound and legally mine.

The Board of Trade sometimes asked for clarification and/or valuation of the declared items and, on one occasion, I was asked to send photographs. Naturally the authorities had no idea who I was, or what I was about. I stressed to them (and anyone else who was prepared to listen) that I was only interested in the artifacts from the historical point of view and that there was not enough money in the world to persuade me to part with even the most trivial artifact. I often felt aggrieved that divers had gone on 'my' wreck and removed artifacts without declaring it to the local Receiver of Wreck, an illegal act, and my legal and honest activities cost me time and money. Over the years I have probably spent thousands of pounds on equipment, travel, accommodation, boat fuel, research, postage, photocopying, etc., in pursuit of my little project, and the only reward I sought is knowing I have done my best under the circumstances to gather as much information as I could on the life and times of the *Dryad*, and record it for posterity.

I thought it might be a good idea if I identified myself to the authorities in London. I telephoned them and asked if they would like to see some of the items that had previously just been lists of declared artifacts. To my surprise they said they would. So on the appointed day I set off for town laden down with as many items of interest that I could pack into a large hold-all. I do not think I am breaking the Official Secrets Act by disclosing that I brought the proceedings at "HQ" to a complete halt. The director and his surprisingly small staff ceased normal work for a couple of hours while they pawed over the artifacts, and I entertained them with stories as to how each came to be found. They very kindly said they had enjoyed my visit. I know I had.

I do not know why, but ever since I started diving on the *Dryad*, the one thing I always wanted to find, (apart from the ship's bell that is), was the captain's pocket watch and chain. Right at the beginning of my 1990 diving holiday, my dream might have come true. I say 'might' because I cannot be certain.

At the beginning of each trip to Start Bay, I mentally ranged over the wreck site, thinking

"ALL I SAID WAS THAT WE WANTED £131.07 FOR HIM TO KEEP THE RING!"
FIRE
ACME AIR
BRIAN SCUTT '04

of areas which had been excavated; those which had been fully investigated, and those which may still be productive, in that an especially difficult piece of concretion may have been left in the past, usually at the end of a long, tiring, chilly and unproductive weekend's diving. Such an area was in the middle of 'Captain's Cabin Gulley' close to a piece of the lower deck. The inverted 'T' shape of a piece of deck and hull side, plus the frame of the hull sometimes produced a catchment area for artifacts which might otherwise be randomly distributed. In this particular case, the small corner was covered by a gin wheel, a cast iron spoked pulley wheel used to load and unload cargo. The presence of this wheel further reduced the space available to work, but I had had good 'vibes' about this area for a long time.

The overburden had been lowered by a foot or more by the previous winter's gales and the wreck site was fairly exposed. I was easily able to waft down to the frame as a starting point for chiselling. Depending on the type of concretion, it is sometimes better to hit debris direct with the flat of a heavy hammer, and this is what I did this time. It sounds drastic, I know, but there is no other way of breaking up the solid mass of stones, coal fragments and pieces of iron, etc, all cemented together. I always stopped every few hammer blows and wafted away the clouds of 'dust' created, so I could examine the area just cleared. Sometimes I disturbed worms and the friendly wrasse come in and gulp them down.

Plates 39 and 40
Photographs showing (left) a gin wheel and other ironwork concreted on the sea bed and (right) a large wrasse taking advantage of excavations amongst cringles to expose worms and other food items.

After some twenty minutes work I saw the glint of brass, and a few gentle taps exposed the square corner of an object as yet unidentifiable. Almost on top of this lock, for that is what it turned out to be, was a piece of mussel shell, with the mother of pearl glistening in the sunlight. I have been fooled too often in the past into thinking that bright shiny shells were some wonderful items of jewellery. One has to estimate the size of an object before it is fully exposed, and a few more exploratory taps with the hammer showed the brass item to be about five inches square. Gently chiselling around it revealed a very nice door lock, with the ring handle resting on top; the connection bolt having rusted away long ago. I noted that the lock had the maker's name and address stamped on it, "J H & H Menk" Hamburg, probably indicating it was fitted in Hamburg during one of the *Dryad's* visits there. Again my mind wandered back a century or so, imagining the carpenter obtaining and fitting a new lock. I know that the lock was fitted and was not just on a shelf in the stores as the 'tongue' of the lock was broken off (I had found it a year before in a different area) and the lock was in the locked position when I opened it up for cleaning.

As I worked I noticed that the piece of mussel shell seemed to have got bigger and more rounded, but in the gloom I could not see clearly, (apart from the problems with close focusing associated with middle age). It must be an oyster shell, I thought, as they are flat and round. As I peered at it, it seemed as though there was a sort of rim around the edge. A 'pot lid' , no doubt, as I have found these on other wrecks and the metal often remains bright and shiny, protected by the paint coating, until disturbed. Selecting a fine chisel I tapped away the concretion under the lock and after a few more minutes it came free, taking with it some more material from near the edge of the 'pot lid'. I did a little more tapping, and a little more wafting. A couple of inches away from the 'pot lid' there appeared to be a piece of twisted wire, or maybe fine chain. As luck would have it, the concretion here was fine and fairly loose and I was able to expose more of this new item of attention by rubbing it with my gloved fingers. It definitely was a piece of chain, and as I lifted it up it ran back towards the 'pot lid'. A gentle tug and the 'pot lid' rose up, except that it was a pocket watch! The mother of pearl appearance was the coppered metal backing for the face, together with a fragment of the remaining enamel. Blackened with age and still covered with bits of cemented shell and coal dust, battered from storms and the like, but clearly a watch nevertheless. The chain was still firmly attached and of course ran vertically downwards. My respiration rate had risen considerably at the thrill of my find, and on checking my air I was dismayed to discover I only had a little left. As I chiselled downwards my work and breathing became more frantic as I did not want to leave my prize on the sea bed. I carried on until my contents gauge showed zero and I was having to suck hard. I had to surface. My wife was acting as boatman in the inflatable and breathlessly I told her of my find. I can almost hear the tut-tutting from some diving readers who, having learnt to dive by numbers, always have to surface with a third of a tank of air. In this case the anchor was literally by my side and just twenty feet of rope separated it from the boat, so I felt justified in the circumstances of using all my air. I could not remember how much air I had left in my 'empty' tank. A quick swap of bottle and demand valve and the answer was 11 Ats. Normally I would never dream of fitting a bottle on with such little air, but I had to try. Trying to conserve my air as much as possible, I sat in the boat for a few minutes regaining my composure and breathing rhythm. On the bottom again it seemed as though the chain was caught around a number of galvanised iron bolts, doubtless items from the ship's stores thrown there during the wrecking. First one, then two, then three I chiselled around and got free. Still the chain disappeared downwards, and of course I had no idea how long it was, nor whether it was broken or complete. The chain was just a few millimetres away from the frame edge, and I thought if I used my fine-bladed bolster chisel I could cut down against the ship's hull and reduce the chances of damage to my longed for artifact. The air was almost exhausted by this time, but by gentle sipping and trying to keep calm and methodical I chiselled on. A gentle tug seemed to indicate a slight movement. A couple more taps on either side to free a little more coal dust. Air really tight now. You will have to surface now I thought, or you will be down there with the crew for ever. One last tap with the chisel at the back and it came free. Grabbing my bag of tools and my prize I finned for the surface flat out. Never before have I totally exhausted an air cylinder on the bottom, and I hope never to do so again. I placed the watch and chain in a little wet canvas bag I keep for such contingencies and headed back to shore. I did not look at it at all until I reached our campsite. By then it was evening, with just a little light, but I took a photograph to record the scene (Plate 41 – below).

Plate 41
The watch and chain as recovered.

I slept well that night, dreaming of getting back home to see my friendly dentist, who sometimes allowed me to use his ultra-sonic cleaner on my delicate artifacts: and to see the watch in all its glory. When cleaned, the chain proved to be of more interest that the watch. Both items seemed to be of fairly modest value and both lacked any form of hallmark. However, on closer examination the tee bar on the end of the chain was stamped with PAT.FEB.20. 1872. Stamped inside the back of the watch were the letters HCF and numerals 53380. These may be makers number and initials, but there was no other identification. The silver was more of a yellow colour than the bright colour typical of English/sterling silver; together with the lack of hallmark suggests a non English origin. Regrettably the steel workings of the watch were largely corroded away.

I have examined several photographs of Captain Thomas with his watch and chain and only one shows any similarity to the one I recovered from the wreck. This is the photo of the captain with his wife and child. I would love to think it is the one I found, but the photograph is not that clear, although it has to be said that the pattern of both is unusual, featuring a double link.

Plate 42 and 43
The watch and chain
after cleaning.

Clearly, life on board did not suit the wearing of jewellery, but in port maybe small items may have enhanced the somewhat drab appearance of the sailors, in particular the officers. One such find in the early days was a silver pin with a spiral groove running down it, typical of a jewellery or tie/cravat pin. Sadly, the jewel or whatever was missing. I say this not because it may have been valuable, but personal items like this may have been marked with a name or initial, helping me to identify the owner; such as with Carl Lange's ring.

When one views a film or play at the cinema or on television, the 'props' are artifacts contemporary to the age in which the scene is set. They help to bring alive the action. This is especially true of bygone eras, where the props/artifacts are unfamiliar items today. A shipwreck is rather like a time capsule since, under the right circumstances, whatever was on board the ship at the time of the wrecking remains there on the sea bed, unless and until it is removed or rots away. Thus the artifacts recovered from the *Dryad* help to recreate a vessel of her period.

A great deal of development and technology has evolved in the 100 years plus since the *Dryad* was lost, and the relatively crude artifacts often bring home the extent of these changes and progress. Imagine for example, no power of any sort on board save that of the muscle power of the seamen; just sails to propel the ship around the world; a candle or oil lamps the only lighting. It is amazing what was achieved with what they had. Some things have changed very little however. The remnants of cutlery and crockery show that they would not be out of place in a ship, or indeed home, of today.

Traditionally, many metal fittings on board sailing ships were made of brass. Not only was it virtually corrosion proof, but when polished it was very attractive to look at. Today brass is relatively expensive, and for some items modern materials like stainless steel and plastics have replaced their yellow metal forerunners. Because of its ability to resist corrosion, much of the surviving artifacts are brass or brass based. Ship's scuttles (portholes), stair treads, lamps and fragments of them, deck light fittings, hinges, rail supports, taps, keys, locks, navigation instruments, binnacle base fragments, steering wheel fittings, screws, nails, tags, buttons, bearings, bullets, pump parts, sink plugs, cuphooks, clock parts, . . . they all emerged from beneath the surface of the sea bed. Some items just appeared in the gloom as soft overburden was wafted away, but others had to be slowly teased out from their concrete coffins to be admired again in the Devon sunlight a century after entombment.

In the nature of things, as seamen were hired usually just for the duration of a single voyage, the *Dryad* had only the captain as a permanent member of the crew. Thus the possessions the men had with them were usually minimal but artifacts, which were overtly personal belongings, were always the most poignant to me. The remains of small penknives, buttons from their clothing, the odd coin from their pocket, all were pathetic reminders of the harsh lives which were snuffed out one night many years ago.

Chapter Eleven

ARTIFACTS – THE GALLERY

If one reads the specifications of an iron sailing ship, it will be seen that these fall under two main headings; the principal dimensions, ironwork and general outfit, which together make up the main body of the vessel and which I largely dealt with in Chapter 4; and the inventory of outfit and stores, which might be considered the more interesting as it covers the more personal items.

These listings would be expected to be kept in the offices of the builders, but it will be remembered that in the case of Thomas Royden and Sons, the builders of the *Dryad*, these were destroyed by fire in 1879, five years after she was built. I did not expect to find any lists; nor did I.

For any reader keen to read such a list (and they do make good reading), I can recommend the specification of the iron ship *Abeona* in David McGregor's excellent book "Merchant Sailing Ships 1850–1875". Although built some years before the *Dryad*, she was essentially similar in most respects.

So my list had to be constructed from items found on the sea bed, or fragments of same. Where artifacts have a story attached to them I largely related to these earlier in the book. However there are many items which may be of interest to the reader and help bring the ship to life. I have illustrated these below, together with explanatory captions.

1 Steering wheel boss and centre spoke cap (when the latter is at 12 o'clock position, the rudder position is dead ahead). This helps the helmsman to position the wheel more readily while steering. Although relatively common to have the boss engraved with name and port of registry, by no means was this a universal practice. In my case it enabled me to identify the *Dryad*.

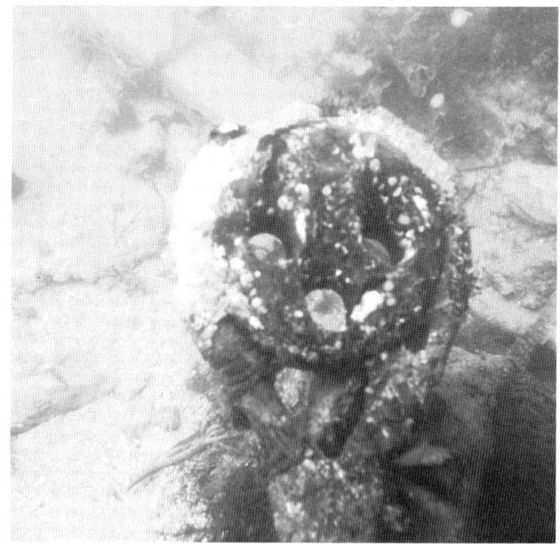

2 Dead Eye made of lignum vitae used to attach the lower masts to the side of the ship by chain plates via lanyards, usually made of hemp rope. The upper Dead Eyes were bound to the wire shrouds by parcelling and serving – making a smooth covering to prevent chafing.

3 Fairlead. A massive iron moulding fitted to the top edge of the deck to allow the smooth passage of mooring ropes between ship and shore, or between ships in port. This one (from the stern starboard quarter) was heavily corroded. Note the deck edge worn away, and some of the numerous white bricks found scattered all over the wreck site.

4 This object was quite a puzzle when first found, so I turned for help to the National Maritime Museum in Greenwich. As always they were really helpful. I quote from their letter: "this is almost certainly a rail socket used to house the heel of an ensign pole . . . the flanges were counter-sunk into the upper and lower faces of the capping rail and held in position with screws on each flange. The squared ends were necessary to prevent whatever was inserted into the socket from turning". So imagine the *Dryad* sitting majestically in the water, proudly flying the red ensign from her stern with base of the pole fixed into this socket. The dive where we recovered this artifact sticks in my memory for a number of reasons. It was the earliest dive in the year, the clearest visibility I can remember and the last dive I had with David Light. Scale – 1 cm divisions.

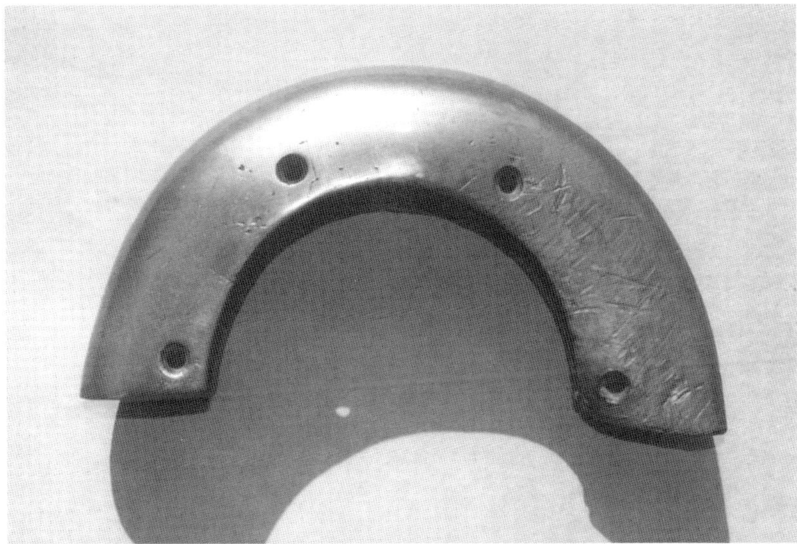

5 The poop rail is a transverse handrail supported by upright banisters separating the poop deck from the main deck below. There are a set of steps at either end of the rail connecting the two decks. Both ends of the poop rail are capped by the 'u' shaped brass casting illustrated. Some of the crew are leaning against the poop rail in photograph plate 16. Note the deep scratches in the cap due to wrecking.

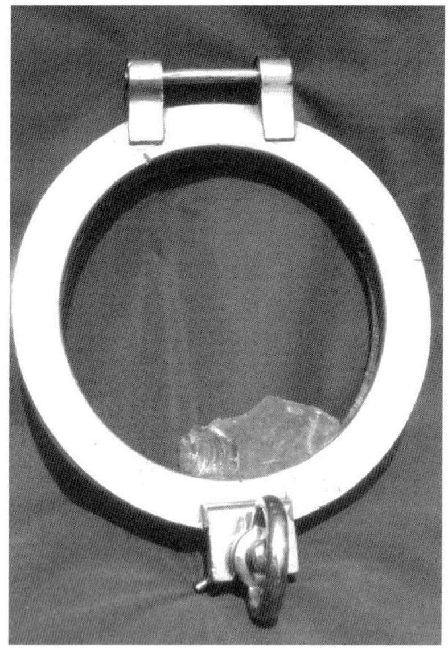

6 Portholes; or more correctly shipside scuttle with turnbuckle to hold scuttle closed in rough weather or open in calm weather for ventilation. *Dryad* had seven on either side at the stern, in the captain's and officers' quarters. Sometimes ships' scuttles were fitted with frames of brass but the *Dryad's* scuttles were fitted with galvanised iron frames. In the two examples here the frames have all but corroded away. Note the polished scuttle protected by being buried under the overburden, the second scuttle 'sand blasted' by exposure. Note also the oval shape, deformed by force during the wrecking.

7 Various sized sheaves out of pulley blocks usually made of lignum vitae, the bearing (see 8) of brass. Pulley blocks of different sizes and groupings, single, double and treble. Examples seen in ship's rigging from Plates 11 and 12. Blocks on the sea bed often disintegrate as they are usually held together with an iron strap and built up with blocks of wood.

8 Roller bearings (brass) for sheaves in pulley blocks.

9 Ornamental stair tread (for steps leading down to saloon), plus anti slip tread for top of wash board – the latter preventing a surge of water in a rough sea from going down the companion way.

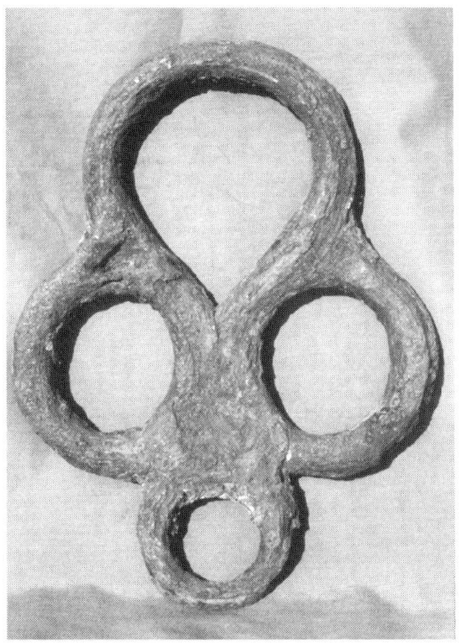

10 Cringles. At their simplest these were strengthening rings of material (often of galvanised iron, but with small sails sometimes rope) fitted into the sail edge or corner to provide attachment points for the ropes/chains (the sheets) to control the sails. They were usually named after that part of the sail which they occupied. Examples here: spectacle clew irons (a), sail hanks (b).

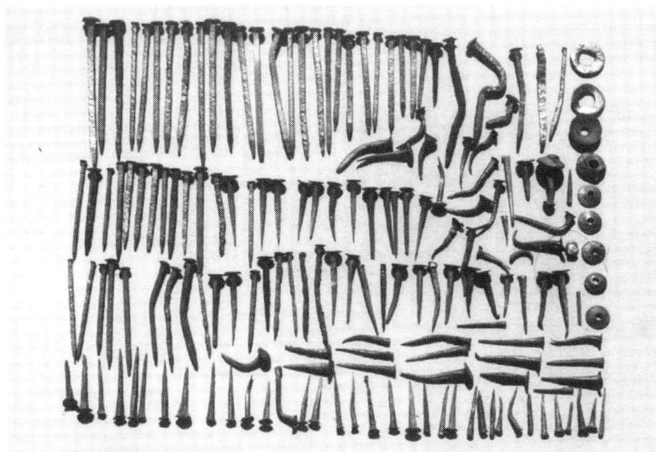

11 Copper nails, rivets, roves, pins and tacks – most probably associated with ship's boats rather than the ship herself.

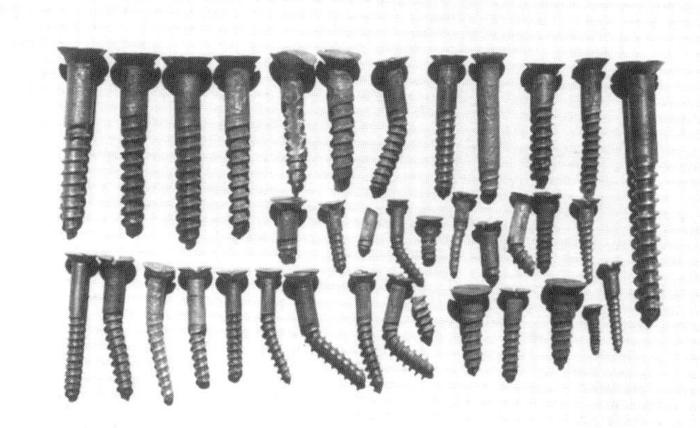

12 Variety of brass screws – note range of dimensions.

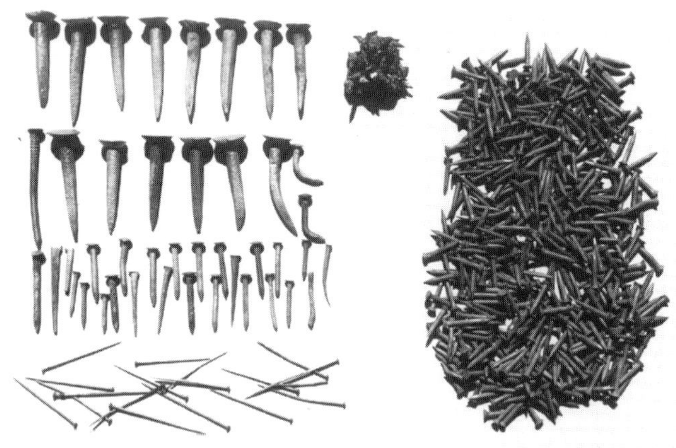

13 Brass nails, tacks and pins. Heap of small nails were found as a solid concreted lump (as small sample in top centre) probably originally in a small bag or sack.

14 Deck light surround. The poop deck being solid wood had a number of deck lights – a triangular section thick glass lens set flush in the deck allowing light through to the saloon or cabin below.

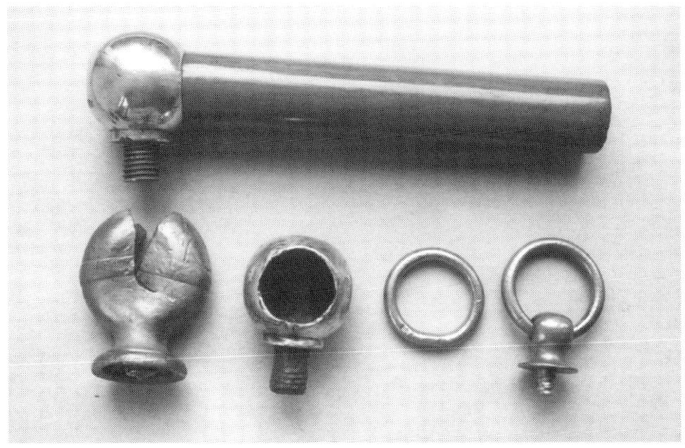

15 These brass balls house the ends of wooden and rope hand 'rails' fitted to sides of companion ways to steady the passage of crew walking along/up/down at sea, especially during rough weather. Note the crushed ball and imagine the forces required to do this during the wrecking. The rings (right hand side) also hold ropes for support.

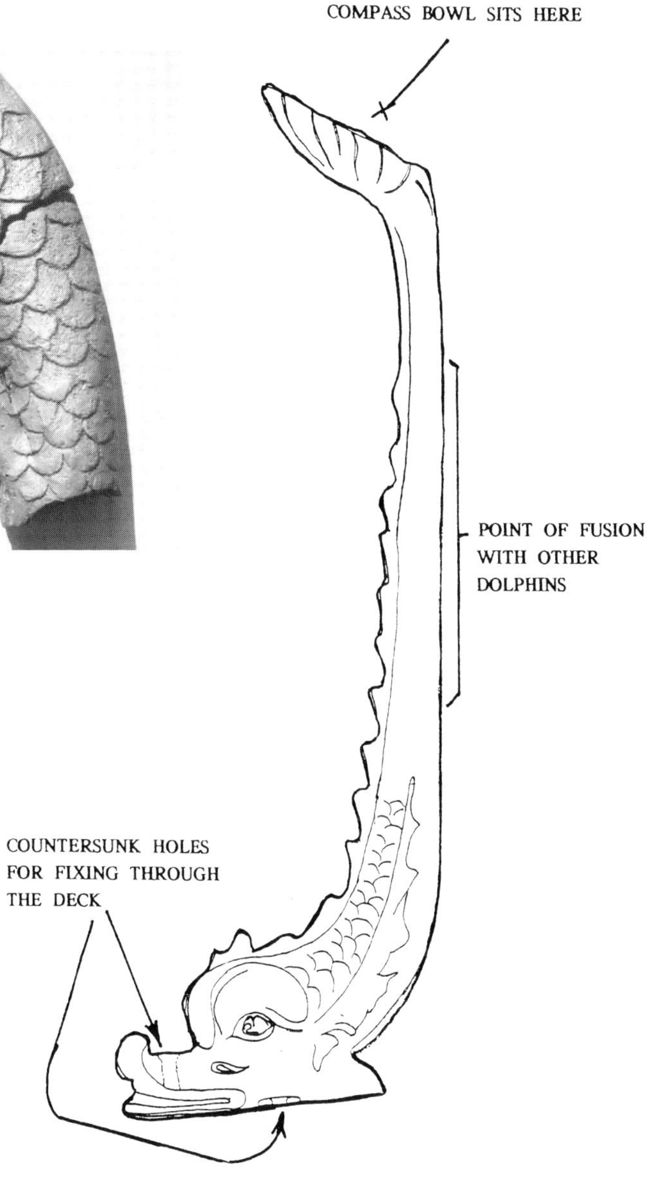

COMPASS BOWL SITS HERE

POINT OF FUSION WITH OTHER DOLPHINS

COUNTERSUNK HOLES FOR FIXING THROUGH THE DECK

16 These are fragments of the ship's dolphin binnacle. A binnacle is a non-ferrous column, situated just in front of the steering wheel, bearing the gimballed ship's compass with lights either side. The fact that the *Dryad* was equipped with such a fine ornate cast brass unit reflects the overall quality of the ship; lesser vessels may have had a wooden binnacle. The illustration is of a similar single dolphin, drawn from one of a triumvirate, in the possession of a friend; but not as pleasing as the one on the *Dryad*.

17 Saloon skylight opening handle/latch. Allows ventilation into the saloon during calm weather.

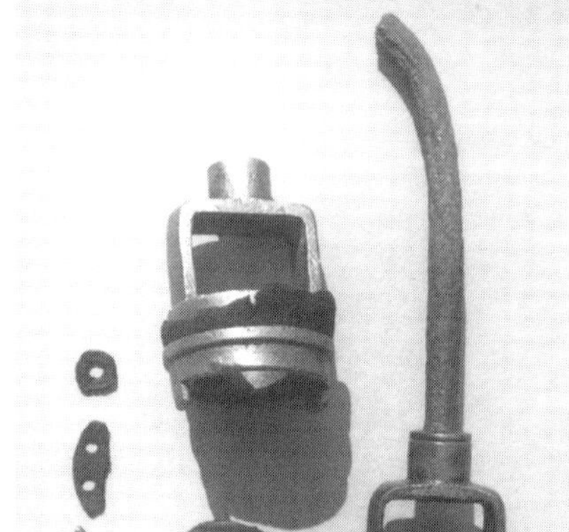

18 A pair of water pumps 2½" diameter. These are too small to be the main or bilge pumps, but are likely to be for washing the decks, cleaning, rinsing and flushing the galley with salt water. Fresh water was far too precious to be used for such purposes at sea.

19 Pieces of yellow pine decking plus a dead eye, on sea bed, exposed when overburden wafted away.

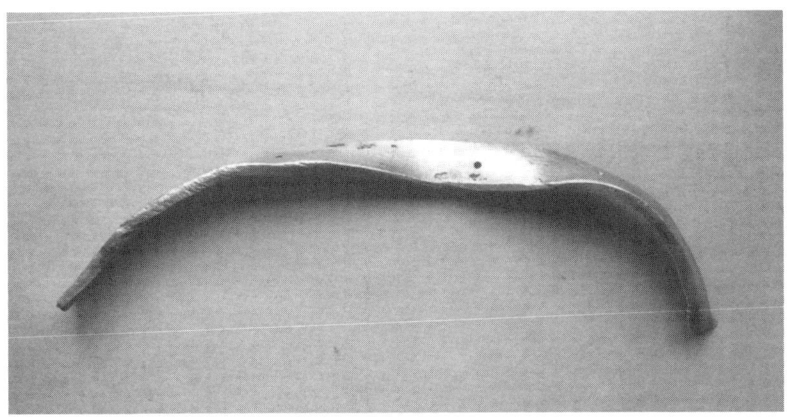

20 Brass binding hoop from base of wooden quarter deck bucket (the main deck buckets had galvanised hoops). Buckets dropped over the side on a length of rope obtained small quantities of sea water for washing, rinsing off, firefighting, scrubbing deck; in short, where small quantities of non-fresh water were required.

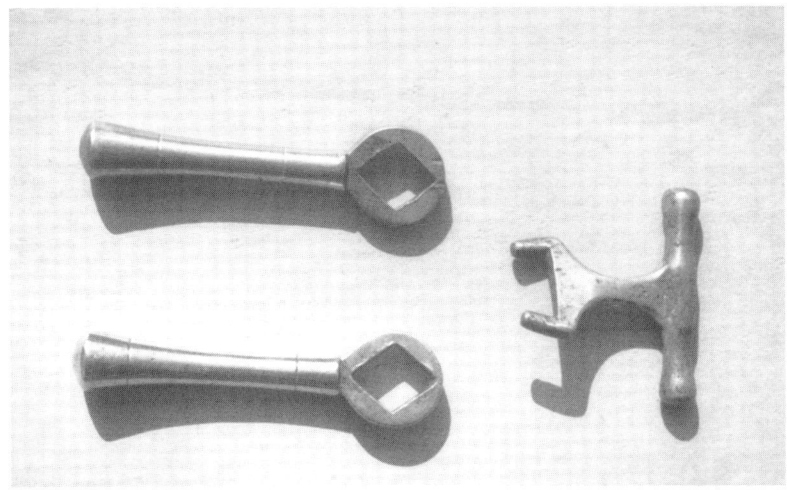

21 A pair of tap handles (so that the contents of the tank fitted with a tap, such as 22 below, cannot be obtained without the separate handle – a form of simple lock). Peg spanner or key normally used to fit and remove a flush fitting cap or similar set into the deck.

22 Brass tap fitted to bottom of grease tank or similar. It was still full of grease on recovery and the leather washers were still pliable.

23 Two brass door locks and latches with outer handle (ring) making easier handling in wet weather, and inner handle (knob). The larger of the two locks was stamped 'J.H. & H. MENK, HAMBURG.' as suggested elsewhere probably fitted by the carpenter to replaced damaged unit during one of a number of numerous visits by *Dryad* to that city.

24 Padlocks and pieces of same. The padlock top right of photograph is stamped 'TOWER & LYON N.Y.' strongly suggesting this was purchased whilst the *Dryad* was in New York, similar to the door lock bearing the stamp 'MENK HAMBURG' being obtained and fitted in that city. All sorts of locks on board ship were specified as having to be made of brass. The padlocks may have been used by crew members to lock chests or cupboards, or by officers to secure hatches against pilfering.

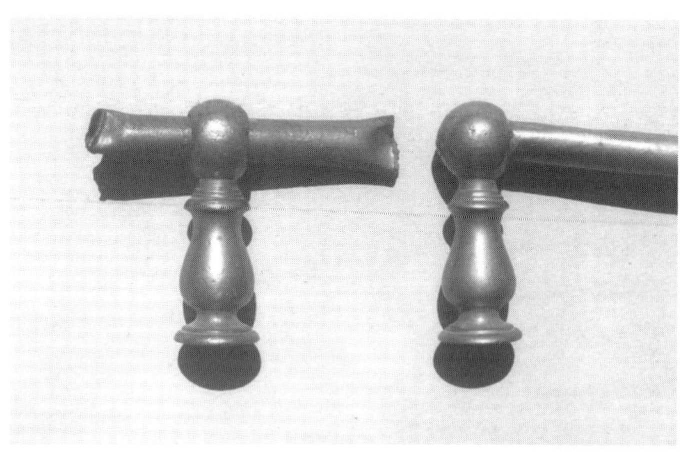

25 Fiddle rail – brass, base showing signs of chromium plating. Used to stop objects from sliding off stoves, sideboards, etc.

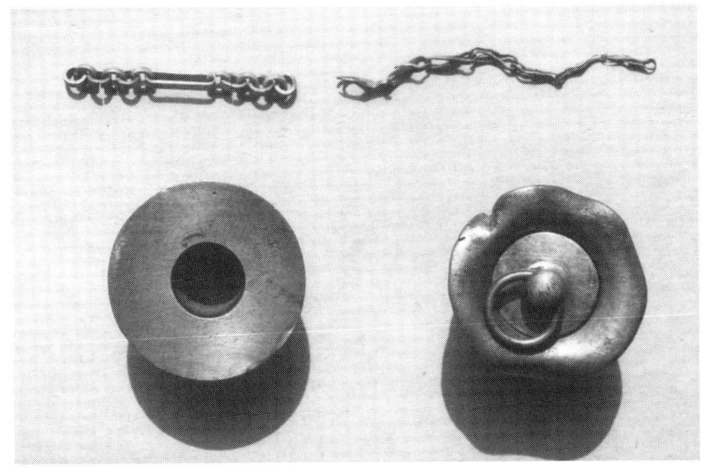

26 Sink and basin plugs and chains.

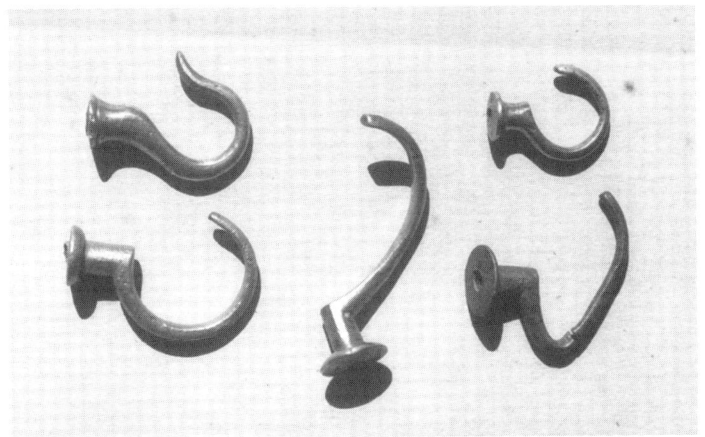

27 Brass cup hooks or similar.

28 Various parts and pieces of oil lamps.

29 (a) Gimballed candle lamp, likely to be fitted to bulkhead in captain's cabin or store.

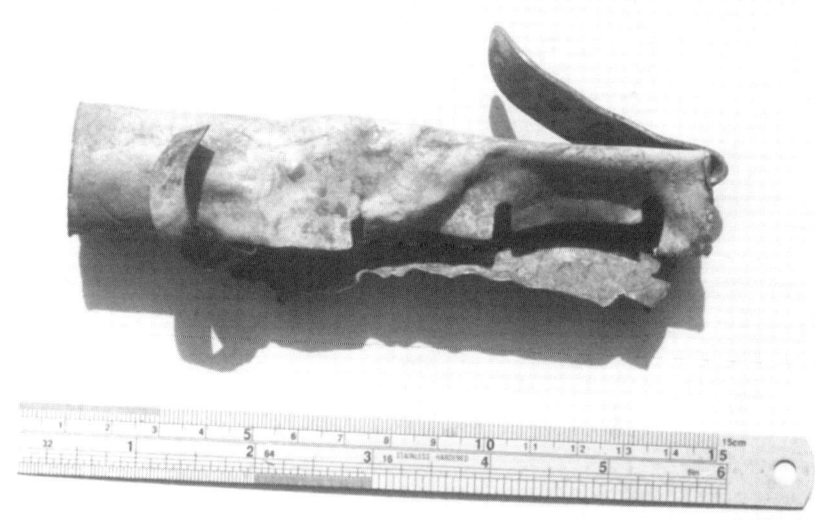

29 (b) Simple candle in brass tube, raised by sprung lever to fit in notches as it burns. Sailors 'night light'?

30 Brass tags. These were used to identify keys to various locks. The WC tag could stand for many things. It is tempting to think of this as the lavatory (water-closet) but this is unlikely as that term would not be used on board a ship and why would a lavatory be locked anyway? Workshop chest is a strong possibility. The second tag CAR SHOP I think is for the carpenter's shop, to prevent pilfering of tools and/or goods.

31 Various ironmonger's tools. From top: combination adjustable spanner and hammer; side right: 2 chipping hammers 1lb 12oz (800 gm) and 12oz (350 gm) for removing rust, etc.; bottom right: caulking iron for sealing seams in decking, etc., with oakum; bottom left: large nail 7½" (20 cm).
Side left: cold chisels.

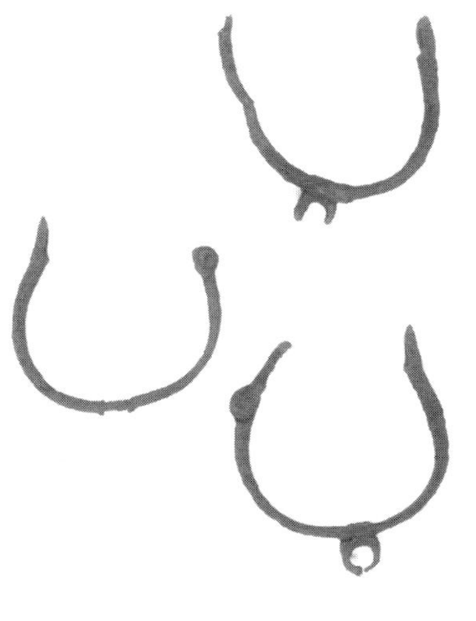

32 One and a half pairs of handcuffs in iron/steel heavily corroded.

33 Fire hose connector.

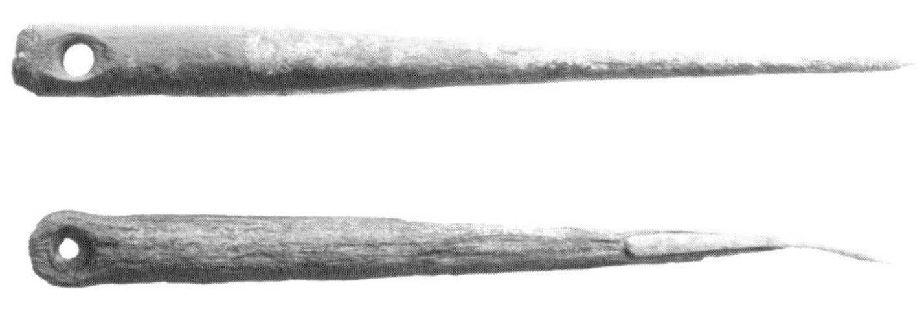

34 Marlin spikes. These are really like giant sewing needles and are used in the splicing of ropes, both fibrous and wire, to form an eye, join two ropes together or stop a free end from fraying.

35 Pieces of wooden handled knives, pocket/penknife, file handle and bottle top with hand cut cork to fit, probably to hold some oil or similar material in the workshop.

36 A series of bullets. Top: .38 calibre to fit the master's revolver and .22 calibre rifle bullets (probably to shoot birds for meat on long voyages).

37 Fish hook; all ships carried hooks, since fish provide a world wide ready supply of fresh protein.

38 Three sounding leads, one small, two medium. There was a deep-sea lead, much bigger than these, unfortunately removed from the wreck site by a third party. Each lead had a depression in the bottom which was filled with tallow. When this hit the bottom, the particles of the sea bed became impressed into the tallow, so the leadsman could tell the nature of the sea bed, e.g. mud, sand, shell, rock, etc.

39 Eye piece shutter and object lens from a telescope. On left, frame from part of a pair of binoculars.

40 Two pieces (broken) of capillary tubing from a thermometer together with fragments of pen from recording barometer, including (top left) pieces of indelible pencil 'lead' for writing on the recording drum.

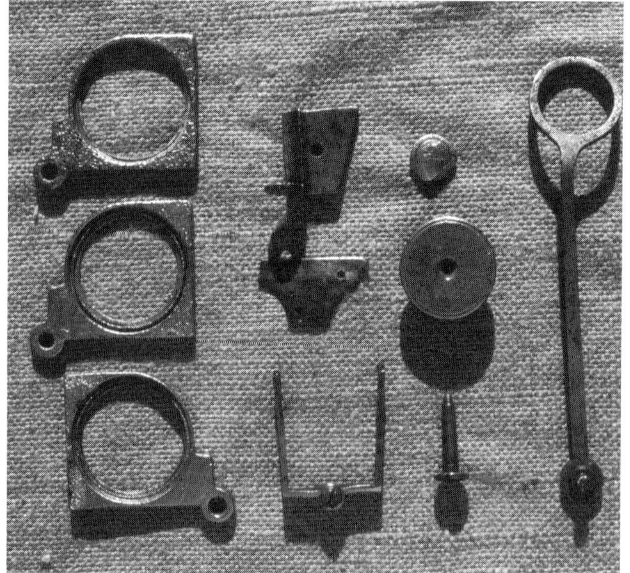

41 Pieces of sextant. Almost certainly the property of Captain Thomas. Vital instruments such as this were too delicate and vulnerable to be in the hands of anyone else; although doubtless some readings were taken by officers and maybe apprentices under close supervision.

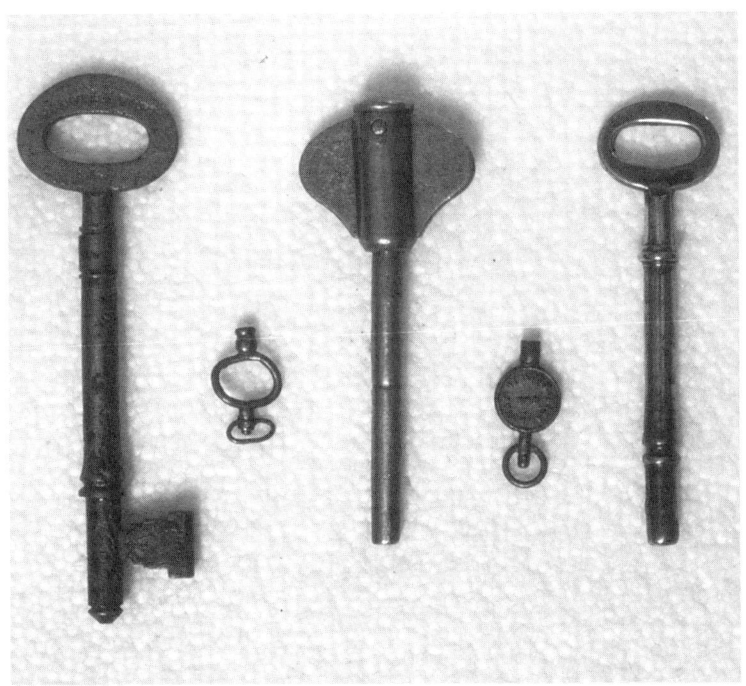

42 Keys. Left and right hand sides are keys to door locks. The central key (called a Tipsey key) was from the ship's chronometer, like the sextant, the captain's own property. It had a mechanism which ensured the key was wound in a particular direction (the reverse of normal). It was in the chronometer box that Mrs Martha Thomas had hidden the love letter to her husband when she left New York, resulting in his reply (undated) but likely from that place (see Chapter 7). The smaller keys are of interest, since the one on the right side is cast "Watchmaker and Jeweller" and the reverse side bears the legend "Jas. J. Dagg, 242, Scotland Road, Liverpool". Could this be the key to the silver pocket watch I wonder?

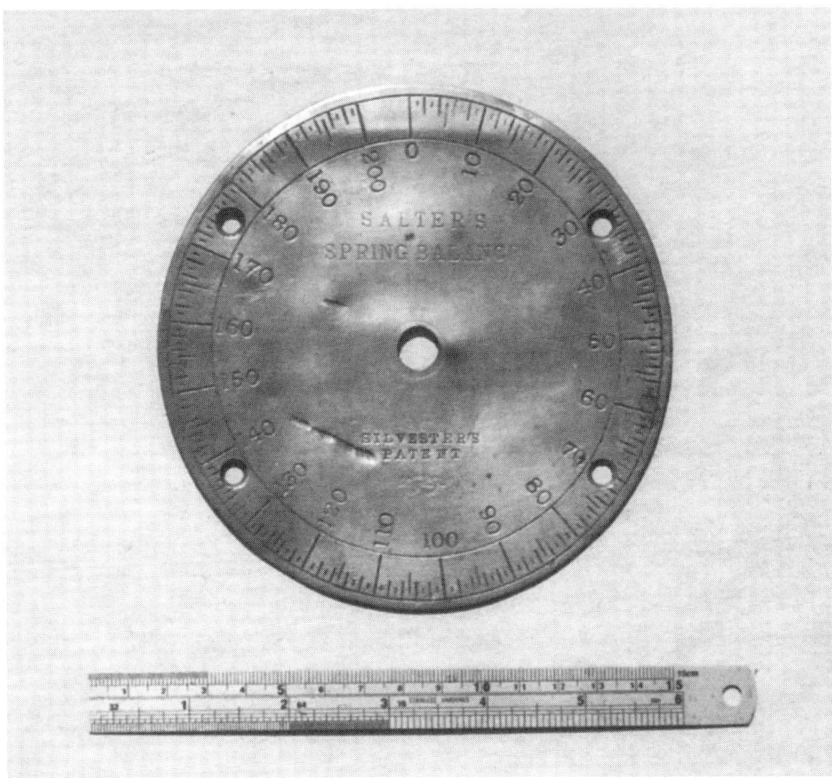

43 Brass dial from 200lb. capacity Salter's spring balance. All iron/steel parts corroded away.

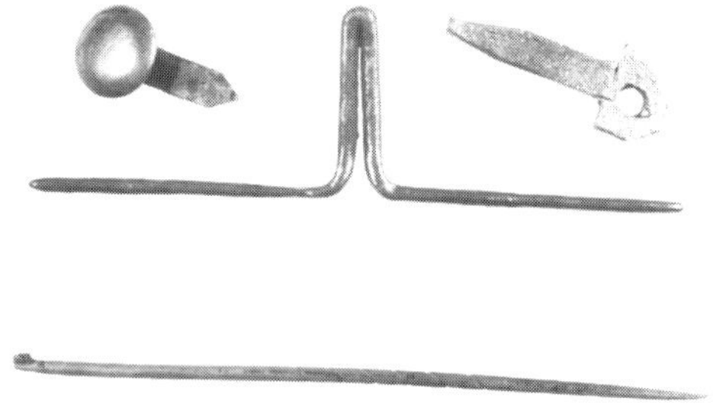

44 Oddments. Top left: a Victorian paperclip; top right: a small pointer cut from sheet brass; top centre: small sliding locking pin from oil lamp door; bottom: a silver stick pin, missing the badge/jewel from the top. Note spiral groove along the length of pin.

45 Various crockery sherds. The variety of patterns suggests the individual pieces were purchased as required and not part of a service at commissioning. It is interesting to note the pieces of heavy lidded pot were typical of the preserves jars containing fruit/jams, etc., given to Welsh sailors by their womenfolk before a long voyage to relieve the monotony of the standard diet (see table 1).

46 Cutlery, ivory/bone handles of knives, white metal, EPNS and silver spoons plus one wire strengthened pewter spoon, white metal and EPNS forks.

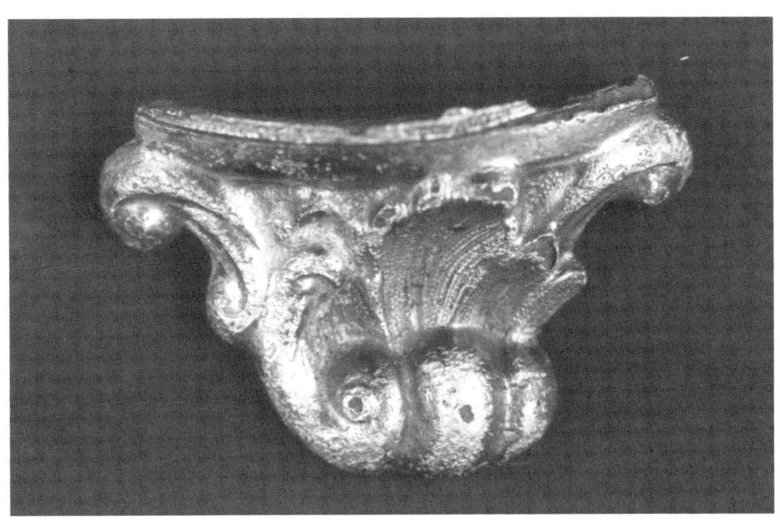

47 The foot from a small silver plated sugar bowl. This would be from the captain's personal equipment and probably restricted to use in port. Such luxuries would not be used by the average seaman.

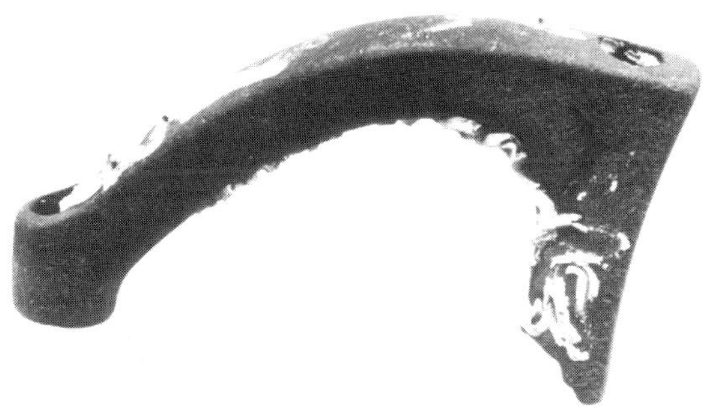

48 Ebony handle from a teapot again probably from the captain's personal property. The white pieces on the outside are worm tubes from the encrusting worm (*Pomatoceros triqueter*).

49 (a) Buttons. There are eight brass buttons from working clothes. Some have inscriptions such as 'NE PLUS ULTRA' (none better) or 'best ringed edge'. One brass button with an anchor motif is from a blazer or jacket cuff. Four buttons made from mother of pearl almost certainly came from the steward's jacket. The button in the centre (a beautiful engraved gold one) and the one below it are solitaires or bachelor buttons, very popular in the late nineteenth century. They were used as a central button of great elegance and bore their name since they snapped together, not requiring sewing skills – a bit of Victorian political incorrectness! Probably the property of the captain or the steward.

49 (b) A separate photo and drawing of a third solitaire with an intriguing motif of begonia leaves and flowers surrounded by a belt and clasp.

50 Scattered over much of the wreck site, but nowhere numerous, these cast iron decorative pieces, approximately 16" long, bearing the royal cypher and have been the subject of much discussion. It has been suggested that they are part of a parcel of cargo, possibly decorative fire-place surround tops, destined for British embassies/consolates in South America via Valparaiso.

51 Parallel ruler. Vital navigation aid which enables parallels to be transferred over maps to calculate positions, both actual and predicted. Illustrated here is the hinge recovered from the wreck, and a ruler belonging to Captain Thomas and loaned by his family.

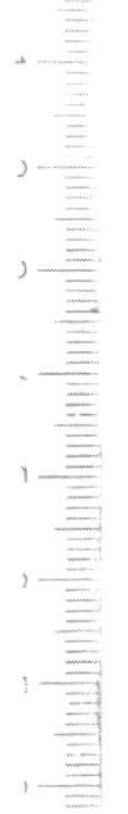

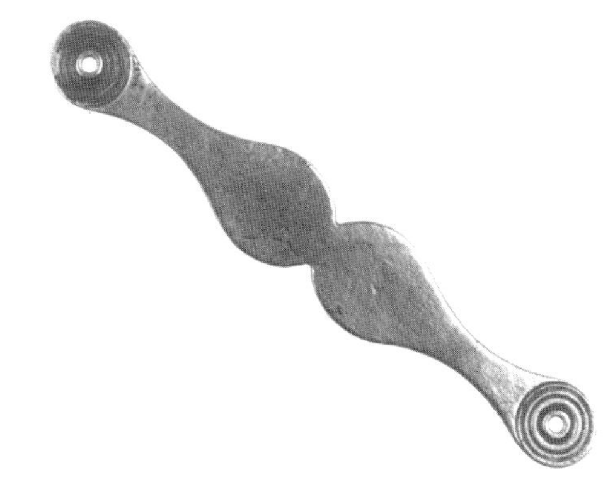

52 Ink well. Fairly rough cast glass, probably belonging to the captain. Would have had a metal cap to stop ink from spilling and/or drying out. The sculptured edges at the base would have held simple pens.

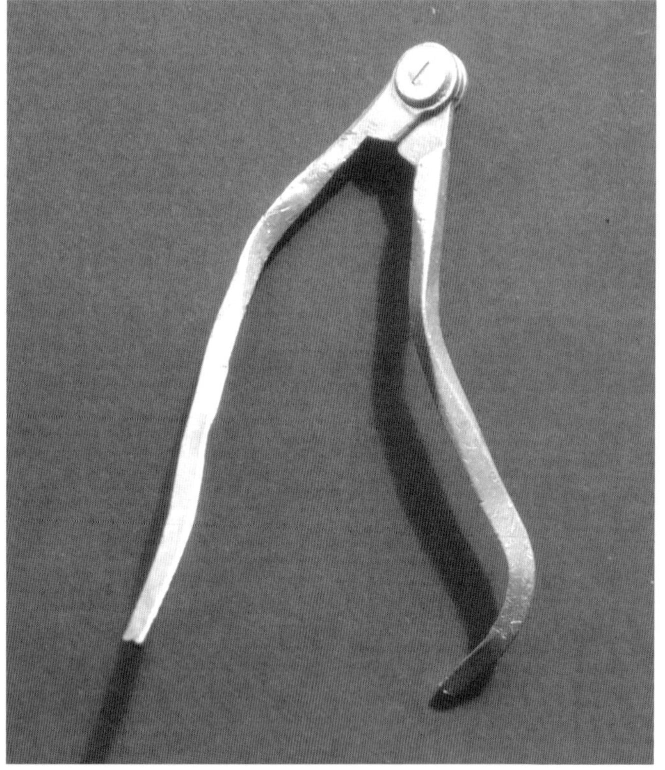

53 Navigator's dividers – an early find. The sharp steel points have long since rusted away and the wrecking has caused them to be bent, but otherwise in good condition.

54 Mrs Mary Jenkins with the hand muff made from albatross skin and feathers.

55 Three pan scale weights, in cast iron. Note the lead 'make weights', so each unit can be adjusted to its exact stated weight.

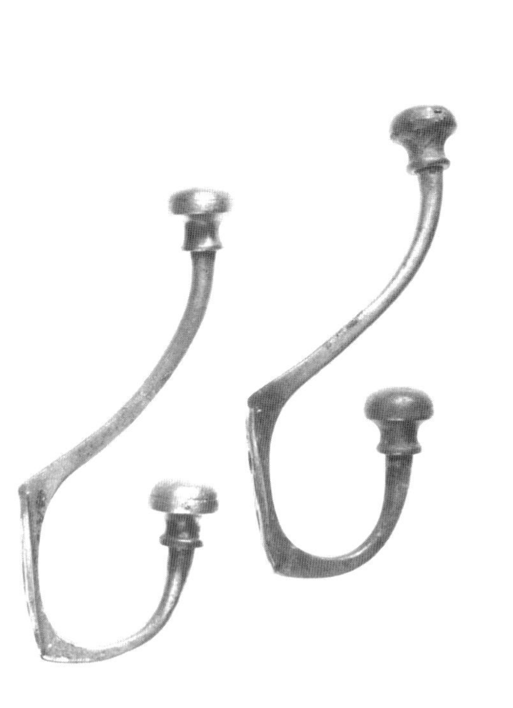

56 A pair of ornate brass coat hooks from officers' quarters. Two of a number found, the others severely worn/damaged.

57 Sherds of port (on the left) and starboard (on the right) navigation lamps. The starboard lamp glass is blue, but together with the yellow flame of the oil lamp behind the lens, the light shows green. The port lamp glass is red, as expected.

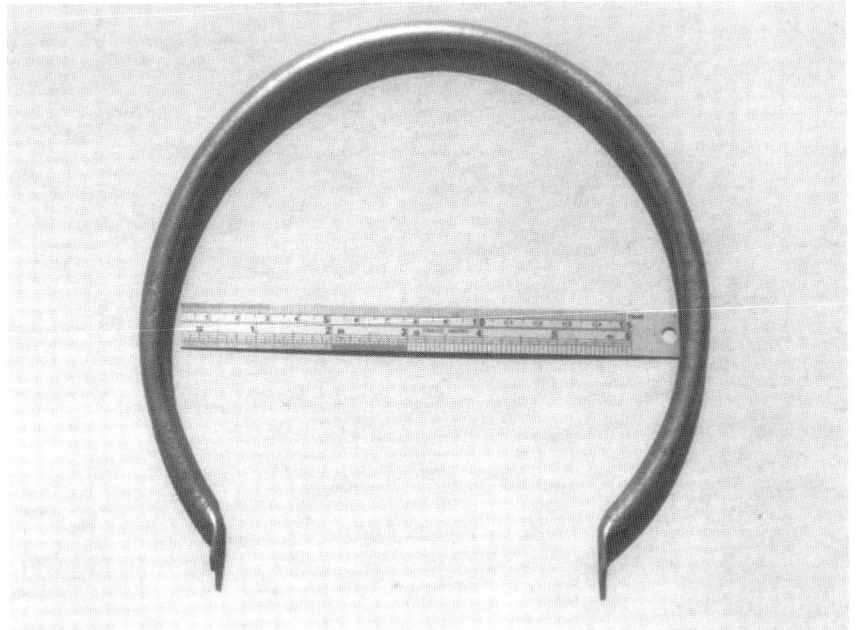

58 Carrying handle from a navigational light.

59 Suspensory ring from a gimballed hanging barometer.

The Revolver (60)

Although you are naturally hoping to find things whilst excavating the sea bed for artifacts, the unexpected sometimes appears. Such was this occasion when I was disentangling some small items of ironmongery – a bunch of clip hooks as I remember. While kneeling on some irregular bits and pieces my neoprene reinforced knee pads had polished some raised edges. Always keen to examine everything minutely, I noticed where I had been kneeling showed a rounded star shape, with brass glinting in the sun. This definitely warranted a closer look. I nearly always wore a pair of canvas gloves over my neoprene gloves as a form of protection from sharp edges of rock and iron. They also came in handy for rubbing over things to clean them. I was astonished at what emerged, for it was the much corroded remains of a (loaded) Smith and Wesson type .38" calibre revolver. This was the standard merchant service captain's issue "to defend the owner's property". I wondered if it had ever been fired?

I suppose it is true to say that most small boys (of all ages) are interested in guns and so it was with me. I used to do a lot of clay pigeon shooting and was vaguely interested in cartridges. I had not heard of those in the revolver (BRAUN & BLOEM) so I took them to show to an expert at a game fair (Mr Geoffrey Boothroyd of the Shooting Times). He was not able to tell me anything about the firm at the time, nor subsequently following a lot of research. Trust the *Dryad* to throw up something unusual. I must admit I did anticipate some fun with the 'powers that be' over my finding a loaded revolver, but nothing happened; they must have realised the effect 100 years of immersion in sea water would cause.

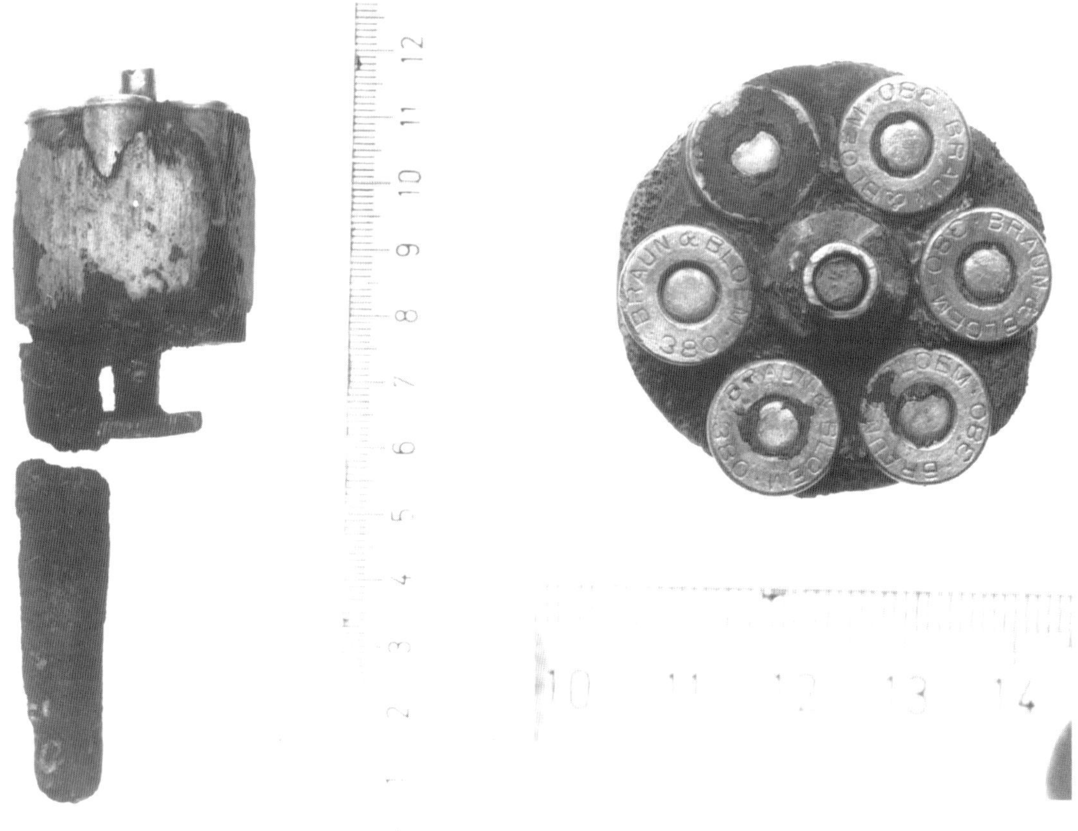

Mystery Objects

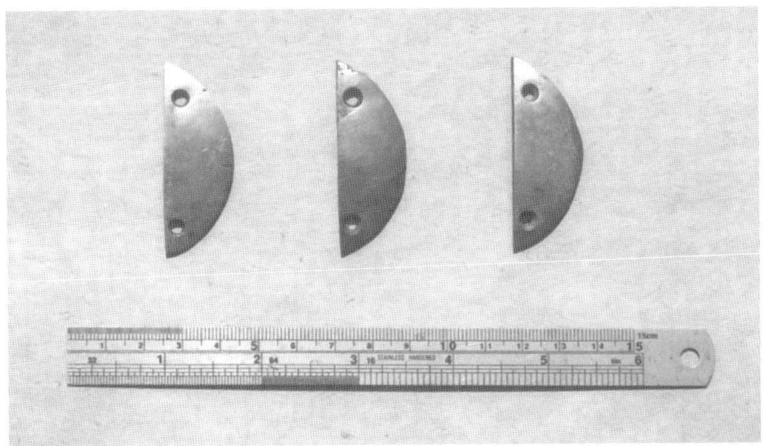

1 What are these? Polished brass one side, they are slightly domed and tapered through. These 'half-moons' have two unusual angled countersunk holes, 60° instead of the more normal 45°. This suggests that the holding screws, or whatever, are designed not to come undone accidentally.

2 Nick-named the 'pepper pot', many people have examined this brass object, but no one has come up with a plausible explanation so far. The mushroom shaped cap is solid brass and has a very fine female thread which fits the male thread on the cylinder top. The two springs were fitted either side of the 'piston', which bears an angular groove round it, maybe a seal of some sort. Maybe this had perished, since none was found in the artifact. The 'piston' was a sliding fit in the cylinder, and had four large holes drilled through it, approximately the same diameter as the solid rod. Maybe this is a damper of some sort? There is no sign of any means of attachment to anything though.

3 Another mystery object which seems as though it is made to slide between two runners, or perhaps around a trapezoid stem. It is a shame it seems to have nearly half one side broken off.

EPILOGUE

John Bankes Walmsley died at his home 'Hartfield', Allerton, on Thursday, 30th July 1896. He was 67 years old. He was buried in the family vault at Childwall Church on Monday, 3rd August. There was a large attendance of general mourners as well as family and representatives of staff of J B Walmsley & Co at the funeral, together with a large number of wreaths.

The will was published in October 1896, and was entirely in favour of his family. He left £166,354–15–2d. nett, a sum which by today's standards would have made him a multi-millionaire.

Thus in the space of just three years the two firms of Royden and Walmsley had ceased to exist as builder and owner although there was still maritime involvement through the Royden family with the Indra Shipping Line.

In the preceding pages I have done my best to be as accurate as I can be, where possible, by going to the original data. Some of my information has been derived from newspapers and great care has been taken here as any inaccuracies are frequently duplicated in further reporting as others pick up on the story.

Throughout I have used imperial as opposed to metric measurement, as I have written of the ship and her equipment in the measurements of her time. Most people still think in, and imagine in, imperial measurements. So please bear with me if you are a metric thinker; I have included a small conversion chart for your convenience in the Appendix.

I do not claim to be an expert on any subject covered by this book, but have done my best to tell the story as it was uncovered. If I have made any mistakes then I apologise. I just hope you have enjoyed reading it and share with me the pleasure I have derived over the years diving and researching the *Dryad.*

She has been a large part of my life and although I no longer dive, it gives me a great feeling when I look towards Start Point and think of her remains lying there.

Dryad, I salute you.

GLOSSARY

AFT	The rear or back end of the vessel, nearest the stern.
AIR	Compressed atmospheric air, breathed whilst diving.
ATS	Abbreviation of the term atmospheres, used as a measurement of pressure within the container for the air (cylinder, tank, bottle) and thus contents of same.
ARTIFACT= ARTEFACT	A man made object as distinct from a natural thing.
BALLAST	Heavy material placed in the bottom of the hull to counterbalance the weight of the mast and spars. Traditionally stones, gravel or iron but nowadays usually water.
BARQUE	A sailing vessel with three or more masts, square rigged on all except the mizzen, which is usually the aftermast and is fore and aft rigged. The *Dryad* was rigged thus in the latter years of her life.
BEAUFORT (Scale)	A table divided into 12 divisions from zero (calm) to 12 (hurricane) force winds, to indicate wind conditions.
BELAY	To secure (make fast) a rope around a fixed point such as a cleat or a belaying pin.
BELAYING PIN	A cylindrical pin of wood or metal, fitted through a hole in special racks, for example the main rail or fife rail, to which ropes may be attached. There may be as many as 135 on a full rigged ship. Occasionally used in brutal regimes to beat sailors.

BILGE	The rounded part at the bottom of the hull close to the keelson (inner keel) inside the ship. Often contains water slopped aboard plus additional debris of various origins. Sometimes lined with cement to reduce wear and tear and reduce acidic corrosion.
BINNACLE	A wooden or non-ferrous column or pillar which carries the ship's compass and its illumination for night viewing.
BITTS	Heavy bulks of timber fixed to ships decks for securing cables. (The 'big boys' version of a sampson post!)
BLOCK	A group of several or a single pulley/s to lead a rope in a particular direction, or when used together with others to gain a mechanical advantage.
BOW	The front of the vessel (cf the stern).
BULKHEADS	Internal walls of the vessel, dividing it into separate compartments. Often strong constructional elements and usually watertight.
BULWARKS	The sides of the ship above the deck and waterline. Usually topped by the main rail. Offers limited protection from rough seas to sailors on deck.
CAPSTAN	A mechanical device for lifting great weights such as anchors. A large cylinder or barrel, vertical in position, driven by large horizontal bars inserted into the top of the device, and walked round by gangs of sailors. Sea shanties were often sung to aid the toil.
CAULKING	A means of sealing the gaps between planks or decking using teased fibres of hemp rope driven in by a caulking iron and hammer, then sealed with tar or pitch.
CEMENTING	A layer of cement mixture covering the bilge or internal decking for protection.
CHOCKS	Wedges used to stop a weighty body rolling about in the hold when the ship is in motion. Also small pieces of timber wedged between the coaming top clips and the covering tarpaulin to keep the hold watertight.
COAMING	Short vertical wall around the edges of the hold, hatches, door sill, etc, to prevent deck water going through the opening.
COMPANION HATCH	A covering with door or doors and often a sliding roof to permit access to accommodation below.
CHAIN PLATE	Secure area for attachment of the shrouds on the side of the vessel.

CHART HOUSE	A room close to the bridge where charts and the like may be laid out for consultation and where navigational instruments are kept.
CLEAT	A wooden or metal device secured to the body of a ship with a pair of opposing wings or horns around which a rope may be belayed.
COMPRESSOR	A device for filtering and compressing breathing air into cylinders.
CONTENTS GAUGE	A device for measuring the pressure and therefore amount of air left in a cylinder.
CYLINDER	Alternative name for tank or bottle which holds the air.
DEMAND VALVE	Mechanism invented by Jacques Cousteau and partner to enable the diver to breathe air freely at whatever depth (and therefore pressure) he/she is at.
DEPTH GAUGE	Device for measuring ambient water pressure and therefore depth. (Approximately 10 metres = 33 feet = 1 atmosphere = 14.7 lbs sq inch).
DRAUGHT	The depth of water required for the vessel to just float, that is the distance between the bottom of the keel and the water surface, measured vertically.
FAIRLEAD	A fitting with a single or sometimes double 'U' shaped channel through which a rope (particularly a hawser) is fed to the outside, usually for mooring purposes.
FIFE RAIL	A hardwood or iron rail fitted around the base of a mast pierced with holes to take belaying pins, to which running rigging is secured.
FINS	The flattened extensions worn on the feet for propulsion. Often vulgarly called 'flippers'.
FO'C'SLE	Abbreviation of FORECASTLE, derived from fighting ships of old where there was a castle fore and aft housing soldiers, and from where they fought. Latterly a small raised deck at the bow, and generally housing the ordinary crew and sometimes livestock.
FULL RIGGED SHIP	A sailing vessel with three, four or five masts each rigged with square sails.
HALLIARD	Ropes used to hoist and lower sails, spars and flags.
HAWSER	A thick rope used for mooring or towing and having a looser construction, the greater amount of elasticity allows for some degree of shock absorption.

HEAVE TO	Resetting the sails in order to stop the ship.
HELMSMAN	Person at the wheel who steers the ship. In difficult conditions there may be two or more people at the wheel.
HOLD	The internal space into which the cargo is stowed.
INFLATABLE	The name given to a relatively small boat constructed of tubes of strong flexible material made rigid by inflation with air. Stable and virtually unsinkable, thus very popular with divers. Powered by outboard motors. R.I.B. or RIB: an inflatable made rigid by use of stiff flooring as an integral part of the craft.
MASK	A watertight rubber shield bearing a face plate of strengthened glass which contains air, worn over the upper face and eyes in order to allow the proper refractive indices between water and eyes allowing clear vision.
MASTER	The commander of a merchant vessel, used interchangeably with Captain.
NEOPRENE	A type of artificial rubber containing numerous tiny bubbles of nitrogen used in the manufacture of diving suits. Those which allow ingress of water are called wet suits; those which largely exclude water are called dry suits.
OAKUM	Teased fibres (usually old hemp rope) driven into cracks and crevices and spaces between planks, sometimes tarred, to provide waterproofing. Maybe then sealed with pitch (distilled tar). (See also CAULKING).
OVERBURDEN	The loose material lying at the bottom of the sea. Often in motion with the movement of the water.
PORT	The left hand side of a boat or ship when looking towards the bow. Port light shows red.
RIG	The arrangement of a vessel's masts, spars and sails; e.g. ship rig, barque rig, etc.
RIGGER	One who is skilled in organising and fitting the masts and spars.
RUNNING RIGGING	That part of the rigging which moves as the positioning of the sails are moved. (cf. standing rigging).
SCUPPERS	Apertures or pipes fitted into the sides of the ship at deck level to allow drainage of the deck of seawater.

SHEETS	Ropes holding down the bottom corners of the sail and used to control (trim) them.
SHROUDS	The lower and upper standing rigging, from the outside of the ship's hull to the topmast.
SPEAKING	Communication with another vessel at sea, usually by means of signal flags.
STANDING RIGGING	That rigging which is used to hold upright the masts etc and not move as does the running rigging.
STARBOARD	The right hand side of the ship when looking towards the bow. Starboard light shows green.
STAYS	Rigging supporting the masts in a fore and aft direction.
STERN	The back end (aft) of the vessel (cf. the bow).
TANKS	Alternative term for cylinders/bottles as air containers.
VICTUALS	Ships' provisions, especially food.
WINDLASS	Simple form of winch, rather like a horizontal capstan, but much less powerful. Operated via pump action ratchet mechanism by a few seamen via moveable bars.
YARDS	The transverse spars which carry the square sails on ships rigged thus.

APPENDIX

Conversion table

Length centimetres (cm)	cm or inches	inches (in)
2·54	1	0·394
5·08	2	0·787
7·62	3	1·181
10·16	4	1·575
12·70	5	1·969
15·24	6	2·362
17·78	7	2·756
20·32	8	3·150
22·86	9	3·543
25·40	10	3·937
50·80	20	7·874
76·20	30	11·811
101·60	40	15·748
127·00	50	19·685

Mass (Weight) kilo-grams (kg)	kg or lb	pounds (lb)
0·454	1	2·205
0·907	2	4·409
1·361	3	6·614
1·814	4	8·819
2·268	5	11·023
2·722	6	13·228
3·175	7	15·432
3·629	8	17·637
4·082	9	19·842
4·536	10	22·046
9·072	20	44·092
13·608	30	66·139
18·144	40	88·185
22·680	50	110·231

kilometres (km)	km or miles	miles
1·609	1	0·621
3·219	2	1·243
4·828	3	1·864
6·437	4	2·485
8·047	5	3·107
9·656	6	3·728
11·265	7	4·350
12·875	8	4·971
14·484	9	5·592
16·093	10	6·214
32·187	20	12·427
48·280	30	18·641
64·374	40	24·855
80·467	50	31·069

tonnes (t)	t or UK tons	UK tons
1·016	1	0·984
2·032	2	1·968
3·048	3	2·953
4·064	4	3·937
5·080	5	4·921
6·096	6	5·905
7·112	7	6·889
8·128	8	7·874
9·144	9	8·858
10·161	10	9·842
20·321	20	19·684
30·481	30	29·526
40·642	40	39·368
50·802	50	49·210

Area hectares (ha)	ha or acres	acres
0·405	1	2·471
0·809	2	4·942
1·214	3	7·413
1·619	4	9·884
2·023	5	12·355
2·428	6	14·826
2·833	7	17·297
3·237	8	19·769
3·642	9	22·240
4·047	10	24·711
8·094	20	49·421
12·140	30	74·132
16·187	40	98·842
20·234	50	123·553

Volume litres	litres or UK gallons	UK gallons
4·546	1	0·220
9·092	2	0·440
13·638	3	0·660
18·184	4	0·880
22·730	5	1·100
27·276	6	1·320
31·822	7	1·540
36·368	8	1·760
40·914	9	1·980
45·460	10	2·200
90·919	20	4·399
136·379	30	6·599
181·839	40	8·799
227·298	50	10·998